Passion of the Slave Girls

Passion of the Slave Girls

Heroic Stories Based on Historical Records

Edward N Brown

Crystal Sea Press
Chicago, IL

PASSION OF THE SLAVE GIRLS

Scripture quotations in this work are taken from:
The New American Bible, Revised Edition, Copyright © 2010, 1991, 1986, by the Confraternity of Christian Doctrine, Washington, DC, and are used by permission of the copyright owner. All Rights Reserved. No part of the New American Bible may be reproduced in any form without permission in writing from the copyright owner.
The New American Bible, Copyright © 1970 by the Confraternity of Christian Doctrine, Washington, DC, and are used by permission of the copyright owner. All Rights Reserved. No part of the New American Bible may be reproduced in any form without permission in writing from the copyright owner.

ISBN: 978-1-7367712-2-8
Library of Congress Control Number: 2021904294

Published by Crystal Sea Press, Chicago, IL
CSP
Printed in the United States of America

For information about this title, or to order other books and/or electronic media, contact the publisher at: www.crystalseapress.com

PHILOSOPHICAL/SPIRITUAL SETTING

They were marginalized, denigrated, and persecuted

But they valued Faith and Freedom above all

These are the stories of the unsung heroes – remarkable women of unbelievable strength, courage, and virtue – who gave up their lives for their faith and their freedom – who found eternal love, peace, and joy as saints in heaven.

The holy women martyrs – slave but free –
they climbed the highest ladder and paid the highest price –
they must not be forgotten.

But take notice!
Similar stories continue today in many different forms and disguises – some subtle, some severe – as new and malicious vilifications against faith and freedom continuously rear up all over the world.

Let the past be both a comfort and a warning!
Assaults on faith and freedom, under all sorts of pretenses, are here and now – and will not go away. The saints in heaven bear witness, and the saints on earth are accountable.

Vigilance is key!
Heroes will rise to resist the threats against faith and freedom.
Are you one of them? What is your story?

IN THE BEGINNING was the Word,
   And the Word was with God,
   And the Word was God.
He was in the beginning with God.
All things came to be through Him ...

John 1:1-3

GLORY BE to the Father,
   And to the Son,
   And to the Holy Spirit.
   As it was in the beginning,
   Is now,
   And ever shall be.
   World without end.
Amen.

The Gloria Patri
A Catholic Hymn of Praise
(also called The Minor Doxology)

CONTENTS

PREFACE

THE book in your hand is not a history book or a modern-day inspirational. Rather, it is a collection of stories, yarns, and snippets, based on actual historical records, of events that challenged the spiritual fortitude of the very first Christians – their freedom and their faith – as well as the perseverance of the Christian religion itself. As such, it is both documentary and encouragement in nature. The purpose is to REMEMBER, COMPREHEND, APPRECIATE, and LEARN from past events and long-forgotten marginalized people.

Many of these individuals have become saints – evangelists, heroes, founders, benefactors, ascetics – but the heroic female saints, in particular, are represented in this volume. And it is the martyrs – slave martyrs – that are particularly remembered here. Human beings who sacrificed it all for their freedom and their faith – and individuals within our culture that have not always been given full recognition and respect.

The time period of interest is the first 300 years (more or less) after the death and resurrection of Jesus Christ, although many similar assaults on freedom, faith, and human dignity have been repeated throughout all history – and continue to this day in various forms and disguises –

some subtle, some severe. The hope is that by remembering crucial events from the past, and empathizing with the heroic figures therefrom, it will light up our spiritual awareness, and strengthen our resolve to always maintain a vigilance against threats that can affect our future contentment. Because the freedom to willingly put our faith in Jesus Christ, is the only way to salvation and eternal happiness.

Today's issues of racism and women's rights are the modern outgrowths of ancient injustices. The early Christian church was not trying to revolutionize secular society, but it had a major influence on how slave women viewed their roles in life. Their stories must be told so that we can learn from history, and apply that knowledge appropriately to the issues being faced today.

INTRODUCTION

IN this book, the focus of interest is on female martyrs in the years prior to 313 AD, the year in which the Christians were guaranteed freedom to practice their religion by the Edict of Milan, under Roman emperor Constantine the Great. Of particular interest are the martyrs who were also slaves, the people at the very bottom of the social strata, whose stories are both tragic and sad, but illustrate their stamina and determination to win freedom. Both heartbreaking and distressing, their stories reflect the norms of the time. They desired freedom from abuse, overwork, exclusion, and sexual harassment, and Christianity represented one way to get it. The slave martyrs were richly honored by the early church – their stories are touching and moving – their strength and courage were immeasurable – their faith unwavering – and they provided a bit of hope and solace to a fallen world.

The number of unmarried young women martyrs who have been personally identified as a slave is somewhere around 10, but there are many shades of gray here (e.g., distinction between servants and slaves, indentured and contracted, tradition and circumstance, etc.), so the number is very imprecise. Furthermore, such members of large consolidated group martyrdoms are lost to examination.

Very little is known about these forgotten heroes. Their quest for both spiritual and physical freedom was unimaginable to most people today. Marginalized, denigrated, and persecuted, they climbed the highest ladder of all. They truly were of the greatest holiness and virtue, and deserve to be remembered and acknowledged for their 'heroic sanctity' by those of us still on our earthly journey.

ORGANIZATION

AFTER providing the background setting of historical persecution against Christian female slaves, the grand stories of the heroic martyrs are presented – the exalted heroes Blandina, Felicitas, and the Three Sisters, followed by briefer stories of the lesser-known heroes in the next chapter. An Appendix (containing a detailed list of all names) completes the main content of the book.

The stories are based on historical records,[1] but the exact degree of ultimate truth in each story is uncertain because of the uncertain veracity of the author of the accounts, and the manner (and integrity) of preservation (oral tradition, letter, document, etc.).[2] Each story provides a first-hand accounting of events that actually transpired, resulting in severe persecution of Christians, and the martyrdom of one or more heroic figures.

The Stories of the Exalted Heroes

The telling of the stories of Blandina, Perpetua and Felicitas, and the three sisters, Agape, Chionia, and Irene, are in the form of a letter to the religious faithful, by a person close to the action, but not sufficiently close so as to be lumped in with the persecuted group of believers. The letter-writer probably felt some shame in not being able to witness to the level of ultimate sacrifice, and that he had to hide himself under the cover of anonymity (since there was a real possibility that the letter would be intercepted and traced back to the originator – with a high likelihood of extreme repercussions – the writer had to know this, had reconciled himself to the possibility, and was prepared to face the consequences), but he was sufficiently motivated out of love and compassion (both for the people involved and for the faith) to put pen-to-paper and send out a correspondence that the authorities would probably consider inflammatory.[3]

The three stories are at different points in time and at different geographic locations, so it was not the same letter-writer. In reality, each letter-writer was in a different circumstance with different motivations and different persuasions. In addition to the details of the event, the introductory paragraph of the letter would be different in each case based upon the time, place, mood, and background surroundings. However, to avoid a repetitive beginning to each chapter, the letter has been removed from the beginning of each. A generic letter has been created that is equally applicable to both stories, and improves the readability by removing repetitiveness of the chapter opening.

Therefore, the reader should view the three stories as a narrative (in the form of a letter) from a captivated bystander, of a real-life sequence of events, that has been written with the intent to make sure that others become aware of these events, and that they are never forgotten. It is a letter that tells a story from the heart – a story of unbelievable cruelty by men to their fellow human beings – but at the same time, a story of immense personal faith and fortitude by virtuous individuals, and their commitment to their faith under the most deplorable circumstances – a story that truly illustrates both the very worst and also the very best of qualities of the human condition.

SALUTATION AND OPENING OF A LETTER TO THE FAITHFUL

To the bishops, deacons, presbyters, and devoted believers in the holy churches of Rome, Alexandria, Antioch, and Jerusalem; and to the faithful brothers and sisters in all the holy churches scattered throughout Asia, Macedonia, Palestine, Africa, Greece, and Italy:

From an anonymous and humbled servant of our Lord Jesus Christ, fearful of persecution and saddened by the horrific events of the past few days, but determined to preserve the memories of our most holy saints, and to record the truth of what actually happened here unaltered by official reports or unofficial scurrilous slanders:

I write to you with heavy heart, but with conviction that the love of our most holy God and Lord Jesus Christ will overcome the evil that has tormented us, and that the wicked will be forgiven their sins and the heathen will be saved and baptized. I look forward to the day when all souls will live in harmony with God.

But today I am saddened beyond words. Although the path to salvation and resurrection is rocky, and there are many followers of the 'evil one' ready to cause hurt and despair, the Light of our Lord is still bright – and many good souls are prepared to make the ultimate sacrifice for the faith, just as Jesus of Nazareth did. They will be glorified in heaven, but their names and lives should also be remembered here on earth. We must not forget them. As holy saints, they can help us in our quest for righteousness, and our hopes for eternal salvation, peace, and glory with God the Father, the Holy Spirit, and Christ Jesus our Lord.

As such, the events that occurred here, and to which I now relate by my hand, along with the names of the holy souls who sacrificed everything in defense of our most sacred faith, must not be forgotten. The world needs to know and remember what happened here. May the martyrs rest in peace forever.

NOTES

1. Refer to the following for more detailed information:

Herbert Musurillo, *The Acts of the Christian Martyrs* [Oxford: University Press, 1972]

Anthony Schiavo, Jr. (ed.), *I am a Christian: Authentic Accounts of Christian Martyrdom and Persecution from the Ancient Sources* [Merchantville, NJ: ARX Publishing, 2018]

2. In addition, certain literary license was invoked in order to dramatize the story for emotional effect, by both the historical author and the present author.

3. Of course, this is not meant to imply that the letter-writer was male – it could just as readily have been a female writer.

1 THE PERSECUTED

Who, Why, and How?

THE MARTYRS

To their fellow believers, the martyrs came to be viewed as victors over evil and death, and not just as victims of Roman oppression – they were harbingers of hope, ordained by none other than Almighty God. In the bodies of the martyrs, weakness became strength, shame became honor, and earthly death became eternal life.

As the stories of martyrs were recorded and spread from community to community, they fueled the growth of the Christian church. Through the telling and re-telling of their stories, Christians constructed a group identity based on suffering as empowerment, and death as victory. The crucifixion, death, and resurrection of Jesus, the incarnate Christ, served as the quintessential example of such victorious suffering. Jesus lived in the body, taught in the body, suffered in the body, and died in the body. For the early Christians, it was this very human body that was understood to be the conduit between God and human beings. It was no accident that the bodies of the martyrs became the focus of activity in the unfolding drama of the spread of Christianity – a drama that transformed the helplessness of the individual, no matter the rank, into his authority and control of self-determination – and transformed the meekness of the faith into the dominant religion of the empire. In the stead of Christ, the suffering martyr served as mediator between God and the world. In the body of the martyr, death was unmasked as the gateway to eternal life. As Christ's death and resurrection were understood to redeem the world, so too the death of the Christian martyr continued that work of redemption on behalf of Christ. They made the possibility of victory through resurrection, for all who believed, very real. The martyr bore witness to the solidarity between suffering humanity and the trinitarian God, who became incarnate in the life of Jesus Christ. And this witness was effectual regardless of gender.

Martyrs were considered holy persons – consequently, they were highly honored. Although not always possible, noble Christians sought to gather their remains after death, which led to the custom of the veneration of relics; as well as the construction of many shrines, memorials, and holy places organized around the bodies (or relics) of the saints, both women and men.

MARTYRDOM OF WOMEN

IN the forthcoming years of increasing persecution, many women became martyrs, and many martyrs became saints. In antiquity, the human body was understood on a hierarchical continuum. The male sex represented the highest level, while the female sex represented the secondary level. Furthermore, personal virtues were associated with biological sex. The higher virtues (justice, self-control, courage) were considered to be male virtues, while the lesser virtues (gentleness, modesty, chastity) were understood as female. The female martyr faced the challenge of being and remaining female, even as she moved up the hierarchical continuum of virtue, toward greater and greater maleness, and ultimately to Christ. A woman's exhibition of manly virtues proved her superiority to the persecutors. At the same time, her show of feminine virtues reinforced her accepted role in society.

The strength of the martyr, like that of Christ, was revealed in his or her weakness. This is portrayed most vividly in the body of the feeble vulnerable woman who died in the process of mimicking Christ, and professing the faith – and there were many such women. Whether female or male, the martyrs were understood as participants in the drama of redemption. The body of the martyr, no matter how low in social status, served as the vessel through which that martyr became one with Christ. Hence, even one so low on the spectrum as an illiterate, unrefined, female slave, could take a noble part in the salvation of humankind. For believers, such a transformation was powerful. It illustrated that anyone, even the lowest of the low, who suffered for the glory of Christ, would have fellowship forever with God in heaven. The possibility and hope for a new life, one free of inequity, injustice, and pain, was made available to all. Throughout history, the stories of the Christian martyrs have served as beacons of such hope.

The stories of the martyrs come from a variety of sources. Some lived long before accurate historical records were kept, and some are legendary with no way to obtain independent verification. Others are known for their writings or their deeds, and others are only remembered because someone else knew them and recorded the events in their lives. As with life in general, there are numerous sides to every story and discrepancies in every tale. Of course, that is the case with the stories in this book. While there is no intent to write blatant fiction here, the ultimate level of pure truth in each story is known only to God. To be sure, all the saints and martyrs have contributed to the quest of praising and realizing the kingdom of God, both on earth and in heaven. In so doing, they have enriched the spiritual sense and understanding of all who have followed. Their names, lives, and stories must not be forgotten.

THE SLAVES

THE torturing of slaves to obtain trial evidence against their masters would undoubtedly scandalize modern sensibilities. But in Roman society, it was a logical consequence of the position of slaves in the societal hierarchy. As witnesses to the deeds and actions of citizens, slaves knew everything that went on in Rome, but at the same time were totally dependent on their masters and would only speak at their command. Interrogating slaves about their masters was like asking the masters to incriminate themselves. However, physical torture could free slaves from submission to their masters by enslaving them to their own bodies. Then they would speak not to obey their master but to obey the dictates of pain. It was thought that slaves had no disposition, were devoid of moral autonomy, and if they were no longer guided by their masters' will, then they would be led by sensuality and natural instincts/impulses. And as everyone in Rome knew perfectly well, people instinctively sought to escape pain.[1]

However, it should be noted that there were plenty of instances in which the tortured slaves did not give testimony (true or false) against their masters merely to save their own skins.[2] In the end, the Roman courts understood that torture was not always effective as a means of learning the truth of a case: "It is stated in our constitutions that trust should not always be given to torture, but torture should not always be rejected. Torture is a weak and dangerous thing that may fail the truth. Many people have the patience and endurance to be contemptuous of torture. The truth can never be extracted from them. Others have so little patience that they would tell any kind of lie rather than suffer torture." [3]

Many Christians living in the first three centuries expected that the world would end soon – within their own life-time or the life-time of their children. Consequently, they were mostly concerned with the urgent matter of salvation – repentance from former sins, betterment of their behavior, and spreading of the Good News to everyone who was open to listening. They weren't much concerned with changing the world – it was beyond their aspirations and imagination. Besides, questioning a universally accepted institution, such as slavery, could be considered subversive – and that was the last thing they wanted, given society's already perceived notions and concerns about them.

Slaves make their appearance in the Gospels as a matter of course. They serve their masters and perform the tasks expected of them without provoking any protests from Jesus or his disciples. The first missionaries of the Gospel, men of Jewish origin, came from a country where slavery existed. But it existed in a form very different from the Roman form. The Mosaic Law was merciful to the slave,[4] and carefully secured a fair wage for the laborer.[5] In Jewish society, the slave was not an object of contempt, because labor was not a thing to be despised as it was elsewhere. No Jew thought it beneath him to ply a manual trade.[6] The Apostles and disciples brought these ideas and habits of life with them – the Good News – into the new society ('The Way') which so rapidly grew up as the effect of their preaching. As this society included, from the first, faithful of all conditions – rich and poor, slaves and freemen – the Apostles simply pronounced these beliefs when confronted with the social inequalities that plagued the Roman world.

All of you who have been baptized into Christ have clothed yourselves with him. There does not exist among you Jew or Greek, slave or freeman, male or female. All are one in Christ Jesus. It was in one Spirit that all of us, whether Jew or Greek, slave or free, were baptized into one body. [7]

In the New Testament, slaves are admonished to obey their masters, not only those who were kind and reasonable but also those who were harsh.[8] By showing respect and honor for their masters, slaves could ensure that the name of God and the moral teaching of the faith would not be brought into disrepute.[9] Indeed, serving their masters sincerely was their role and obligation. Not only were they to obey when being watched, but they were to always do the will of God from their hearts.[10] It was thus expected that complete fidelity and obedience on their part, would add credit to Christian doctrine and teaching.[11]

Early Christian doctrine accepted society as it is. Directly changing the ills of society was not its policy. Nevertheless, society would be transformed indirectly through the reaching and influence of individual souls. What Christianity demanded from masters and from slaves, was to live in harmony as neighbors – giving and receiving – commanding and obeying – with equity, remembering that God is the master of all.[12]

PERSECUTION OF SLAVES

AGRICULTURAL slaves were numerous in the Roman world. Most of them worked on large farms of wealthy landowners and were often kept in dirty barracks. They were supervised by stewards, who were either slaves themselves, or free-men enjoying the trust of their masters. Their living conditions were tough, and the treatment they received was often cruel. Such slaves normally participated in the common pagan feasts. But they were not allowed to make their own religious choice. And there were no significant attempts by Christian missionaries to convert them.

Many slaves, both male and female, were often sexually exploited. When they were confined to brothels, their conditions of living could be very unhealthy and unpleasant. However, some female slaves became mistresses and concubines of wealthy men, princes, and even emperors. In such cases, they could live in luxury and were even able to exercise some power.

The bulk of Jesus' followers were originally peasants. On a normal working day, they were expected to be laboring as fieldworkers or fishermen, or grinding at the mill.[13] Many owned one or more slaves who assisted them in their workplace and household labors. Ploughing fields and tending sheep were clearly thought to be typical tasks of slaves.[14]

However, as soon as the Jesus movement began to spread beyond Palestine, it underwent a fundamental shift. While Jesus preached almost exclusively in rural areas, after Pentecost, most Christian missionaries, such as Paul and Barnabas, were visiting primarily the important urban towns of the empire. The originally rural movement was quickly transformed into an urban movement, and new converts were drawn from all social strata of the urban population. In addition, the ancient scorn of labor was absent among the believers in the new Christian religion. Converts to the new religion knew that Jesus had been a carpenter, Peter had been a fisherman, and Paul had been a tentmaker. At a time when those who performed manual labor were considered 'the dregs of the city' by the aristocracy, this new mindset was very appealing – and this included the great mass of workers and slaves. A new sentiment was introduced into the Roman world – Christians did not make a spectacle of their laziness or leisurely lounging – they labored in an occupation.

Gradually, some slaves began to join Christian communities. In general, they belonged to one of two privileged groups: the tradesman/artisan-household/urban worker (with maybe a small plot of arable land) – such as Aquila and Priscilla, who were tentmakers,[15] and Lydia of Thyatira, who was a dealer in purple cloth[16] – OR – the regal/imperial household (the so-called 'family of Caesar') – such as those mentioned by Paul in his letter to the Philippians,[17] and the household in which lived Callistus (or Callixtus), the slave of a Christian master, who himself was a free-man of the emperor Commodus.[18] In fact, many of the people who Saint Paul salutes at the end of his Letter to the Romans are actually servants or slaves in imperial households. Those "who belong to the family of Aristobulus" and those "who belong to the family of Narcissus" include the Christian slaves of those two imperial households that were contemporaries of the emperor Nero.[19]

In general, the pagan religion of the Romans excluded slaves from its functions. But the new religion of Christianity proclaimed religious equality for all – in ancient times, a novelty. The Church made no account of the social condition or sex of the faithful. Slave and master, bond and free, male and female, all received the same sacraments. According to Paul: "All are one in Christ Jesus."[20] And before long, clerics and church officials who were once slaves became numerous – even the very Chair of Saint

Peter was occupied by men who had once been slaves.[21] In the Christian cemeteries there is no difference between the tombs of slaves and those of the free, whereas pagan tombs almost always indicated the servile condition of the deceased. Slaves who died as martyrs were often honored in prodigious manner. For example, the ashes of two slaves, Protus and Hyacinthus, who had been burned alive during the persecutions of emperor Valerian in 253-260 AD, were found to have been wrapped in a winding-sheet of gold tissue. Martyrdom eloquently manifested the religious equality of the slave.

To a large extent, the fate of slaves depended upon the wealth and power of their masters. Most owners didn't really care if their slaves had a religion, as long as they did their work properly. Besides, any religion of the slaves would just be uncivilized mumbo-jumbo anyhow, so they thought. But problems inevitably arose when slaves expressed the desire to become Christians. Permission by the master was required before a slave could request membership in another religion, especially since Christianity was a subversive cult. Not surprisingly, there was often tension between slaves desiring conversion to Christianity and pagan masters. Many rejections were followed by further master/slave distancing, retribution, and punishment (often physically harsh).

There was also frequent tension within Christian households. Many slaves who had been allowed by their Christian masters to join the new faith thought that this would lead to a relaxation of their earthly duties. But rarely was this the viewpoint of the master. An explicit countermanding reply to arguments that would give priority to the religious duties of slaves is given in the Book of Timothy.[22] However, it should be noted that some newly converted Christians freed all of their slaves within their lifetimes, effectively depriving themselves of a considerable part of their estate. There are no records of pagans doing this.[23]

Some Christian slaves went even further and expected that they should be emancipated simply because they had become Christians. Slaves in the Roman world could usually buy their freedom with enough money. Of course, very few slaves had this wherewithal, even if they had saved most of their lives. So, many turned to the Christian church communities for the requisite funds. This, in turn, led to further tensions because of all the competing elements desiring allocation of limited church resources.

Taking the desire for freedom to the extreme, some Christian slaves willfully chose to become martyrs. By becoming a Christian, the slave felt that he had no further obligations to his human master when it came to choosing between his earthly and his religious duties. And knowing that this would not be tolerated by the master or the civil authorities, he was actually envisaging freedom through an honorable death.

MARTYRDOM OF WOMEN SLAVES

REDEMPTION for humanity through the suffering, death, and resurrection of Jesus Christ is intricately woven into the fabric of Christianity. The being who suffered and died on the cross is a personal, relational god – a Trinitarian God – who became incarnate and lived and died in solidarity with suffering humanity. The martyr bears self-witness to the solidarity between suffering humanity and God. He/she takes upon him/her self the features of Christ's suffering – like an imitation of Jesus. This witness is independent of gender. Whether male or female, the martyrs were understood to be participants in the drama of suffering and redemption. Even one at the very bottom of the social totem-pole was viewed as being a champion of the faith, and a true witness for Christ.[24]

For believers in the faith, such an image and representation were very powerful. It illustrated that everyone (even someone at the very bottom of the social strata – a slave and a woman) who suffers for the glory of Christ, has eternal fellowship with the living God. In that possibility, hope for a new life, one free of inequity and injustice, was made available to all.

The slave-girl martyr was probably equally motivated by faith and freedom. Salvation and liberty provided her with reasons to escape from the dreadfulness of everyday life. The slave-girl died for faith and freedom, equally threatened. Such a sensibility is found in the accounts of the martyrdoms of the slaves Zoe, Ariadne, Felicitas, Mary, Maxima, and others.

The Deaconesses of Bithynia – 112 AD

In the Roman province of Bithynia (modern day Turkey's northern Black Sea coast), two young maidservants were tortured, and probably killed by the provincial Roman governor Gaius Plinius Luci, known to history as 'Pliny the Younger'.[25] He had encountered a troublesome religious sect in the province and he wanted advice on how to deal with them – and so he wrote a letter to the emperor Trajan in Rome, inquiring as such. What he had learned about Christian beliefs and practices had been acquired from those Christians who apostatized – those who had first confessed their faith, but then denied their faith when confronted with the threat of execution. What he thought he had determined was this:

that they met regularly before dawn on a fixed day to chant verses alternatively among themselves in honor of Christ, as if he was a god. They also bound themselves by oath to abstain from theft, robbery, and adultery, and to commit no breach of trust. After this ceremony, it was their custom to disperse and reassemble later to share ordinary everyday food and drink.

This revealing was so pathetically innocent that Pliny was suspicious of it. He needed to get at the truth of what was going on. One way to do that was to extract it from two slave women who were officials in the movement, called deaconesses.[26] In an infamous letter to Trajan, Pliny wrote, "I thought it the more necessary, therefore, to find out what truth there was in this [the accusation against Christians] by applying torture to two maidservants who were called 'ministers' [an obvious leadership role]. But I found nothing but a depraved and extravagant superstition."[27]

These deaconesses, or female ministers, were very probably slaves since they were called 'maidservants'. Yet they were recognized publicly as Christian 'ministers'. Their witness for Christ must have been outspoken, because they were arrested and endured great suffering and extensive torture, in an effort to get them to incriminate the rest of the church. But they did not recant their testimony to Christ.[28] These noble slave-girls, names unknown, became early martyrs to the cause of Christ.

The Martyrs of Pamphylia - between 127 and 138 AD

A family of Christian slaves in Attalia, Pamphylia,[29] were martyred under the persecution of emperor Hadrian, because their master had commanded them to participate in pagan rituals, but they all refused. In retaliation, they were burned to death. Zoe was the wife of Exuperius (sometimes called Hesperus), and they had two sons, Cyriacus and Theodulus. They were owned by a rich devout worshipper of the ancient pagan Roman gods, named Catullus. Zoe's job was to tend the house dogs and prevent them from biting visitors. She rarely saw her husband as he worked in the fields far from the house. Zoe was stationed near a roadway, and she freely gave of her own meagre rations to those even poorer than herself who passed by.

On the birthday of Catullus' son, a feast was prepared at the house in honor of the pagan goddess Fortuna. Food was sent to the slaves from the master's table, and this included meat and wine that had been sacrificed to idols. The slave family refused to participate and would not eat the food, Zoe being outspoken in the defense of her religion, which forbid such practice. Zoe poured the wine on the ground and threw the meat to the dogs.

When Catullus learned of this, he became incensed and forced the family to submit to torture, hoping to gain obedience. He gave orders to torture the young boys Cyriacus and Theodulus. The brothers were then stripped, suspended from a tree, and raked with hot iron implements before the eyes of their parents, who counselled their children to persevere to the end.

After this, Zoe and Exuperius were subjected to the most terrible tortures. But the family would not relent. Finally, the pagans threw all four family members into a red-hot furnace, where they surrendered their souls to the Lord. As the bodies were burning, it is said that angelic singing could be heard glorifying and praising the Lord.

The Passion of Perpetua and Felicitas – 203 AD

In 203 AD, a group of Christian believers and catechumens were tried, condemned, tortured, and executed, including two slaves, Revocatus and Felicitas. Revocatus and two other prisoners had been scourged before they were thrown to the beasts. It is said that they all rejoiced at having obtained a share in the Lord's sufferings.

Being pregnant in her eighth month, Felicitas was very distressed that her martyrdom would be postponed because of her pregnancy – since, according to Roman law, pregnant convicts were executed only after delivery. She was afraid that she might have to shed her holy, innocent blood at a later time, separated from her Christian companions, and lumped in with others who were common criminals. Her companions in martyrdom were also saddened – they were afraid that they would have to leave behind so fine a companion – and that she would have to travel alone on the road to heaven.

Therefore, two days before the contest, they poured forth a prayer to the Lord in one torrent of common supplication. And immediately after their prayer the birth pains came upon Felicitas. She suffered a good deal in her labor because of the natural difficulty of an eight-month delivery. One of the prison guard assistants said to her, "You suffer so much now – what will you do when you are tossed to the beasts? Little did you think of them when you refused to sacrifice to the emperor." To this, she replied:

> *What I am suffering now, I suffer by myself. But when in the arena and professing my faith, the Holy Spirit will be inside me and will suffer for me, just as I will be suffering for Him.*[3]

And she gave birth to a healthy girl. The sister of one of her companions brought her up as her own daughter. Two days later, Felicitas was executed in the arena.

MARTYRDOM OF UNMARRIED WOMEN SLAVES

THE virgin slave-girl martyr was probably equally motivated by faith, freedom, and virtue. Salvation, liberty, and morality (especially control over her sexuality) provided her with multiple reasons to escape from the dreadfulness of everyday life. Personal control over all aspects of one's life is a powerful motivation – an overwhelmingly powerful drive for some. *The virgin slave-girl died for faith, freedom, and virtue equally threatened.* Such a sensibility is found in the accounts of the martyrdoms of the slaves Seraphia, Blandina, Agathoclia, Laurentia, Flora, Lucilla, Dula, and others.

Seraphia and Sabina – between 110 and 125 AD

There was a Christian family who fled from Antioch in Syria to Rome to escape the persecutions of the emperor Hadrian. However, shortly after arriving in Rome, the parents died and the daughter named Seraphia (also called Serapia or Seraphima) was left to fend for herself. Although offers of marriage were many, Seraphia was drawn to a religious life, and she resolved to consecrate herself to God alone. So, she sold all her possessions and distributed the proceeds to the poor. Then she sold herself into voluntary slavery, and entered the service of a widowed Roman noblewoman, named Sabina.[31] As the slave of a noblewoman, she was safe from exploitation. Sabina and Seraphia formed a bond of mutual respect and understanding, and at some point, Sabina, who had been evangelized by Seraphia, was converted to Christianity, and they became involved with the local Christian community.

However, the comings and goings of the pair with the underground Christian movement did not escape the attention of the local governing officials. Eventually, they were captured, arrested, and tried for confessing to be Christians. Seraphia was denounced as a witch and commanded to do homage to the pagan gods of Rome. But she refused and was handed over to two shameless young men of Egyptian descent, who tried to rape her. But Seraphia resisted so forcefully that the villains despaired, and then to punish her defiance, they tried to set her on fire by placing her over a burning wood pile. But the fire would not injure her body, as she called on the mercy of God. Exasperated, the reprobates appealed to the local judge Berillus for a ruling on the punishment. Believing that she was a sorceress, the judge ordered her to sacrifice to the Roman gods for forgiveness. But Seraphia remained steadfast and refused. By official decree, then, she was beaten with sticks and rods – but she could not be broken. Amazingly, splinters from the sticks struck Berillus in his right eye, and after three days the tormentor became blind in that eye. Still unable to exact a confession, Seraphia was then executed by beheading. Her body was taken by Sabina and buried in her own tomb.

Being of noble birth, Sabina was spared and warned not to pursue this dangerous religion. But she was so disconsolate over losing Seraphia, that she continued to befriend the Christians. Less than a year later, Sabina was again denounced – as a criminal found aiding and abetting the Christians. This time there was no leniency. When the judge Helpidius questioned her, she humbly confessed,

Christ is my God; I adore Him and serve Him; to Him alone I must sacrifice.

With that, she was summarily executed for her faith by beheading – and all her assets were confiscated. She was buried in the tomb that she herself had built, and where she had interred her beloved servant, Seraphia. The two women soon became revered by the local Christian community.[32]

Blandina and the Martyrs of Lyons – 177 AD

One of the worst persecutions Christians faced in the early centuries occurred in the province of Gaul in Vienne, near Lyons, under the reign of Marcus Aurelius. In the year 177 AD, the wrath of the governor, the military, and the populace was exceedingly aroused against a group of Christian believers, including the 90-year-old sickly bishop of Lyons, the deacon of Vienne, and other prominent followers. The entire congregations of two churches were rounded up, their assets seized, and the believers thrown into prison. False charges of orgies, incest, and cannibalism were trumped up and levied against them. Becoming exceedingly indignant and exasperated, the community soon became outraged and demanded confessions and penance. Having these kinds of people in their community, close to their children and homes, was just unacceptable. Those who would not renounce their faith, and accede to the good and proper Roman deities, were punished by torture and execution. Among this group of martyrs were three women: a slave named Blandina, her mistress and owner, and a woman named Biblias.

The mistress was concerned over Blandina's bodily weakness, thinking that she would not be able to withstand the physical tortures and make a bold confession of faith. The other members of the group were also afraid that she would succumb. But Blandina was filled with such power and conviction, that even those who were taking turns to torture her in every way from dawn to dusk, were weary and exhausted. She was hung on a post and exposed as bait for the wild animals that were let loose upon her, hanging there in the form of a cross. But by her fervent prayers spoken aloud, she aroused intense fervor and confidence in those who were undergoing their own ordeals – they were assured and would not waver.

For in their terror with their physical eyes, they saw in the person of their sister, He who was crucified for them – and that all who believe in Him and suffer for His glory, will have eternal fellowship in heaven with God Almighty.

Agathoclia of Aragon – 230 AD

Agathoclia was a young unmarried Christian slave owned by two people in Aragon, Spain, named Nicolas and Paulina, who had left Christianity and converted back to paganism. They regularly subjected Agathoclia to physical abuse, including whipping and battering, not only in an effort to get her to renounce her faith, but also to reinforce their assumed superiority and her inferiority. But she consistently and humbly took the beatings in stride, and repeatedly refused to renounce her faith.

At some point, Nicolas and Paulina decided that Agathoclia needed to be publicly punished and humiliated. So, they had her subjected to a public trial by a local magistrate. They claimed that she was disobedient by willfully not obeying their orders – and she was charged with refusing to pay homage to the gods when commanded by her owners to do so.[33] But once again, she refused to renounce her Christian faith. This caused her to be subject to severe persecution from the Roman authorities, since they believed that Christians disrespected the gods. The harshness of the sentence included having her tongue cut out, in an effort to get her to stop verbalizing her beliefs. But Agathoclia was resolute, and continued to deny her accusers through hand signs and head waving. Consequently, she was given the full punishment of torture, mutilation, and execution. During the proceedings, Paulina poured hot burning coals on her neck, and then, in a fit of exasperation, threw Agathoclia into the fire pit.

NOTES

---

1. *Daily Life in Ancient Rome* [Oxford: Blackwell, 1992]

2. Clive Skidmore, *Practical Ethics for Roman Gentlemen: the Work of Valerius Maximus* [Exeter, 1996]

3. Alan Watson (ed.), *The Digest of Justinian* [1985]

4. Reference Exodus 21, Leviticus 25, and Deuteronomy 15:21

5. Deuteronomy 24:15

6. quite possibly with the exception of the high religious leaders

7. Galatians 3:27-28 and 1 Corinthians 12:13

8. 1 Peter 2:18

9. 1 Timothy 6:1

10. Ephesians 6:5-6

11. Titus 2:9-10

12. The second greatest commandment – see Matthew 22:39

13. Matthew 24:40-1

14. Luke 17:7

15. Acts 18:1-3

16. Acts 16:14

17. Philippians 4:22

18. As such, Callistus belonged to the imperial 'family of Caesar'. Denounced as a Christian, he was sentenced to hard labor in the mines of Sardinia. However, through the intervention of Marcia, Commodus' concubine, Callistus and his fellow Christians in the mines were set free. The letter of liberation was taken to the governor of Sardinia by an imperial messenger named Hyacinthus, who was himself a Christian presbyter. After his release, Callistus returned to Rome and was ordained as a deacon by Pope Zephrynius. In 217 AD, now a free-man, he succeeded him as Bishop of Rome and Pope.

From 217-221 AD, he exercised great influence in important Christian issues throughout the empire. During his reign as pope, the Church witnessed its first antipope when Hippolytus formed his own Christian community against Callistus, who he believed was too lenient on sinners. At some point, he was killed and then thrown into a well, but his body was rescued and today the relics of the sainted pope are located in the church of Saint Mary in Trastevere (Our Lady of Trastevere) in Rome. See: D. J. Kyrtatas, *The Social Structure of the Early Christian Communities* [London and New York: Verso, 1987].

19. Romans 16:10-11

20. Galatians 3:28

21. Pope Pius in the 2nd century and Pope Callistus in the 3rd century

22. 1 Timothy 6:1-4

23. There is a record that at the beginning of the fifth century, a wealthy Roman aristocrat (and later to be ascetic), Saint Melania the Younger, gratuitously granted liberty to thousands of slaves – so many that her estate lawyer was unable to give an exact number – some sources say 8000, but it may have even been more. Reference: M. Cardinale Rampolla del Tindaro, *Santa Melania giuniore, senatrice Romana* [Rome: 1905], p. 221.

24. A person at the very bottom of the totem-pole was the slave-girl Blandina. But she became one of the most heroic martyrs and saints ever. During her persecution and suffering, it was said that onlookers saw not just a woman being brutalized on a stake, but instead they saw the Christ, "He who was crucified for them, in the form of their sister." Paraphrased from: Eusebius, *Church History*, in *Nicene and Post-Nicene Fathers of the Christian Church*, vol. 1, trans. by Arthur Cushman McGiffert, ed. by Philip Schaff and Henry Wace [Grand Rapids, MI: William. B. Eerdmans, 1982].

25. The dating of Pliny the Younger's governorship is uncertain. It is known that he arrived in his assigned province in time for emperor Trajan's birthday celebrations on September 18 in a year which could be 109, 110, or 111 AD. He served a little more than two years and died in office. Thus, the letters could date from 109 to 113 AD.

26. In early Christian baptism ceremonies, catechumens were anointed and baptized naked, with a deacon accompanying them down into the pool of water. In the case of female catechumens, simple propriety would suggest that a woman would perform this task, since the anointing did not involve merely pouring oil over the candidate's head and shoulders, but was comparable to the way oil was used in Greco-Roman bathing and in athletic contests of the period – the oil was rubbed into the person's skin and over their whole body as a kind of quasi-mystical enhancement. When the baptized woman came up out of the water, the deaconess would instruct her in purity and holiness on how the seal of the baptism was unbreakable.

Also, in the case of female Christians who were sick or otherwise homebound, it was proper for a woman to deliver communion (the Eucharist sacrament) to them, since it would usually involve visiting the woman in her bedchambers. See: John Wijngaards, *Women Deacons in the Early Church: Historical Texts and Contemporary Debates* [New York: Herder & Herder, 2006].

27. Betty Radice (ed.), *Pliny Letters, Books I–VII and Books VIII–X* [Cambridge: Harvard University Press, 1969]

28. Other Christians that Pliny had interrogated had recanted under threat of torture, but he could never be certain if they were just telling him 'what he wanted to hear' or the real truth of what was going on. Roman courts understood that torture was not always effective as a means for learning the truth of a case, since many people have the patience and endurance to be contemptuous of torture. The truth can never be extracted from them. On the other hand, others have so little patience that they would tell any kind of lie rather than suffer the torture. See: Alan Watson (ed.), *The Digest of Justinian* [1985].

29. Pamphylia is the ancient name for the fertile coastal plain in southern Anatolia between Lycia and Cilicia, extending from the Mediterranean to Mount Taurus (all in the modern-day Antalya province of Turkey).

30. Herbert Musurillo, *The Acts of the Christian Martyrs* [Oxford: University Press, 1972]

31. Sabina was the widow of a Roman senator named Valentinus and the daughter of a man called Herod Metallarius.

32. In 425 AD, a church was built over the site of the martyrdom of the two holy women, and dedicated to Saints Sabina and Seraphia (but now known simply as Saint Sabina's). By the 13th century, the church became the international headquarters of the Roman Catholic Dominican order. Even today, under the main altar, one venerates the bodies of the two holy martyrs.

33. This was a grave offense because if the gods were displeased, they could cause disasters and catastrophes on the society (draught, famine, earthquake, fire, pestilence, etc.). It was important that they be kept happy by providing the proper respect, reverence, and tribute. People that wouldn't do this had to

be dealt with one way or another.

2 THE STORY OF BLANDINA OF LYONS

Saint, Martyr, Virgin, Slave

<< *Salutation and Opening of a Letter to the Faithful* >>
(see Introduction)

The greatness of the tribulation in the regions of Gaul near the towns of Vienne and Lugdunum, and the exceeding anger of the local heathens against our holy believers, and the sufferings which the blessed witnesses for Christ endured, I am not competent to describe accurately, nor is it possible to detail it all in writing. For with a mighty strength the devil did assault the servants of God, using all sorts of tricks, deceptions, and prevarications. By this, all the local citizens were stirred up against us – not only were we excluded from forums, baths, and markets, but it was forbidden for any of us to be seen in any public place.

But, by the grace of God, the holy believers remained steadfast, enduring all forms of shame and injury – the weak were rescued and the strong stood like firm pillars against the shaking. With courage and integrity, the witnesses for Christ firmly kept the faith, maintaining that 'the sufferings of the present time are nothing compared with the glory that awaits us in heaven'.

At first, we nobly endured all the harms and vices that were heaped upon us by the local citizenry – hooting, catcalls, beatings, robberies, stoning, and everything that an infuriated mob is willing to inflict on those whom they consider to be unworthy and derelict. At length, many of the servants of God were forcibly taken to the police station by soldiers, and brought before the magistrates that had charge of the town. They were questioned in presence of the public, and having confessed to being Christians, they were locked up in prison until the arrival of the governor.

When finally brought before governor Saturninus, he displayed a marked spirit of hostility toward them. However, a local citizen of high moral and ethical standards, named Vettius Epagathus, who had the full measure of love towards God and his neighbors, was very concerned that unreasonable judgments might be passed against the believers. Strong in spirit, eager to serve, and moved with passion, he petitioned for a hearing in defense of the others. His goal was to show that there was nothing ungodly or impious among them. But the jurors in the court were not interested in listening, and the governor, oblivious to his request, simply asked him if he was a Christian himself. And on his confessing in the clearest voice that he was indeed, he also was taken up into the number of the accused, receiving the designation 'Advocate of the Christians', and sent to the prison. He was a genuine disciple of Christ and a role-model for the others.

The first group of arrested believers were then brought in, and the governor announced to them, "You can win the indulgence of our lord the emperor, if you return to a sound mind."

Sanctus, a deacon from Vienne and the de-facto spokesman for the group, replied: "We have not done anything wrong, and we have not been part of any wrongdoing. Our minds are sound. We have never spoken ill to anyone, but when ill-treated we have given thanks in return. This is because we respect our emperor and our empire."

Saturninus interrupted, saying, "We too are religious, and our religion is simple. We swear by the genius of our lord the emperor, and pray for his welfare, as you also ought to do."

To which Sanctus replied, "If you will sincerely listen to me, I can tell you about the mystery of our faith."

But Saturninus was not so inclined. "I will not listen to you once you begin to speak evil things about our sacred rites. Swear to me in the name of our lord the emperor, that you will not do this."

"The empire of this world I know not," responded Sanctus. "Rather, I serve the true God, who no man has ever seen, nor with these eyes can ever see. Honorable sir, I have not committed any theft or deceit – whenever I have bought anything, I have paid the tax. But I know that my Lord and my God is the King of kings and the Emperor of all nations."

"Enough of this prevarication," said Saturninus, "I have heard enough." Then turning to the others, he stated straightforwardly, "You must all cease being of this unholy persuasion."

But Sanctus countered, "But it is an unholy persuasion to torture, murder, and speak false witness, is it not?" (implying that that was the persuasion followed by the Romans).

"Be not partakers of this folly," reiterated Saturninus sternly and impatiently, with the air of intimidation.

Then, another member of the accused named Maturus, a recent convert, said "We fear no one else except our Lord

God, who is in heaven."

He was joined by Attalus, the pillar and foundation of the church in Pergamum,[1] who said, "Honor is to Caesar as Caesar, but reverence is to God as God." [2]

Then Sanctus said simply, "I am a Christian."

"And you still persist in being a Christian?" asked the governor.

"I am a Christian," Sanctus repeated.

"What I am, is what I wish to be," said Maturus.

"And I am a Christian, and wish to be a Christian," stated Blandina, the only woman in the group. And with them, all the rest affirmed the same.

"Would any of you be inclined to reconsider that position?" asked the governor.

Sanctus' answer was short and quick: "In a matter so straightforward, there is no considering."

After a few moments of pondering, Saturninus asked, "What are the things in your suitcase?"

"Books and letters of Paul, a just man."

Then the governor said, "Have a delay of seven days and rethink your answers."

But Sanctus promptly said a second time, "I am a Christian." And with him they all agreed.

Then, after taking a deep sigh, the governor Saturninus read out the decision and sentence to the jurists and onlookers: "Sanctus, Maturus, Attalus, Blandina, and all the rest – having willingly confessed that they live according to the Christian customs, and since after opportunity offered them of returning to the correct and proper custom of the Romans, they have obstinately persisted to refuse, it is determined that they be imprisoned, and then sent to the arena at the proper time to be subjected to the tribulations therein as punishment. However, because the magnanimity of the emperor is boundless, the opportunity to avail themselves of a proper confession that honors the traditions and customs of Rome will remain in effect throughout the period of confinement and punishment."

To which they all replied, "We give thanks to God."

After this, the rest of the accused began to be examined and questioned in groups. Most of the believers were strong in their faith and openly confessed that they were Christians. But some were unprepared and nervous about the repercussions. Of these, about 10 in number renounced their faith, causing immeasurable sorrow among the rest of the believers. But they were not permitted to walk away. All of the accused were confined together (the persecutors hoping to spread dissension among the ranks). However, those who had confessed were worried about the durability of the confessions, dreading that one could fall away and deny his faith because of the pressures.

More and more servants of God were being apprehended daily, filling up the number of the accused. All the pious members of the two churches, together with the founders, leaders, and financial backers, were rounded up and cast in the prison. Even some heathen household slaves belonging to the well-to-do church members were apprehended, since the governor had given orders that all the Christians should be sought out (and the use of informers [finger-pointers] was one way to do this). Urged on by the soldiers and fearing the pain and tortures that the believers were facing, most of the slaves falsely accused the believers of cannibalism, incest, and other crimes which are lawful to mention, or even think of. Of course, no such crimes have ever taken place, but the damage was already done simply by the accusations. When the rumors were spread about, all the people raged against the servants of God like they were the dregs of the earth – any that were formerly temperate in their conduct toward the believers, now became exceedingly indignant and condescending toward them. Thus, the prophecy of our Lord was fulfilled: "Not only will they expel you from synagogues; a time will come when anyone who puts you to death will claim to be serving God!" [3]

Then, over the course of the next few days, the holy servants of God were sent two-by-two into the arena, where they suffered tortures beyond all description. To an exceptional degree, however, the wrath of the people, as well as the soldiers, fell on Sanctus, Maturus, Attalus, and Blandina. The thinking was that if the leaders could be rehabilitated or eliminated, then the rest would fall in line and the problem would go away.

Blandina was the wild card in all of this. Sanctus, Maturus, and Attalus were strong, healthy, and vigorous, but Blandina was weak, ill, and unfit. Being a simple uneducated slave, her leadership capabilities were disregarded. But the spirit of God was extremely powerful in her. For the things that appear to most humans to be ugly and contemptible, may in fact be beautiful and noble to God. Although frail, sickly, unsightly, and worthless on the outside, because of her love for God, Christ gave her the traits of goodness and beauty on the inside – strength, purpose, virtue, integrity, honesty, and morality were hers in abundance. And the righteousness of Blandina expressed its true glory at this sorrowful time.

Her owner (mistress) was one of the accused, and she was concerned that Blandina would not be able to withstand the tortures and maintain a bold confession of her faith, because of the weakness of her body and the meekness of her personality. But her inner strength was massive and soon became apparent to all. For while the rest of the servants of God were afraid of the pain, and of falling away in the faith, Blandina was filled with such upright power, that those who tortured her one after the other, in every way from morning until evening, were wearied and tired, confessing that they were completely baffled at her grit, bravery, fortitude, and courage. When they had no more tortures that they could impose on her, they were astonished that she remained alive, even though her whole body was broken, mangled, gashed open, slashed, punctured, and pierced. The tormentors gave their testimony that only one of the modes of torture inflicted should have been sufficient to deprive her of life, not to mention the excruciating pain and suffering. But the blessed Blandina, like a noble athlete with the power of God, recovered her strength and composure after each torture, and never renounced her faith. At each stage of the tribulations, she would proudly declare, "I am a Christian, and there is nothing vile done by us."

Sanctus also nobly endured all the horrible and ghastly tortures that were thrown against him. The persecutors hoped, because of the continued severity of the tortures, that he would renounce his faith and admit to the unlawful practices. But Sanctus withstood them with firmness – he would not even tell them his own name, nor that of his birthplace or residence, nor if he were slave or free. But in answer to all these questions, he simply said, "I am a Christian." That was the statement he made repeatedly, in reply to every question that was put to him. Because of this perceived arrogance, the governor and the torturers determined that a quick execution was needed. So finally, they affixed red-hot plates of brass to the most delicate parts of his body, and burned him continuously and intensely. With that, the body of Sanctus became charred, misshapen, and limp. But he remained alive, and never recanted his beliefs.

In suffering for the faith, Christ brought about great wonders, destroying the devil, and showing a heroic example to the faithful that there is nothing to be feared when God's love is present – and nothing painful when Christ's glory is imparted. After a few days, the persecutors again tortured the servants of God, thinking that since their bodies were battered, bruised, swollen, and inflamed, if they were to apply the same torture instruments again, this time with the ultimate consequence of death hanging over them, they would be able to coerce them into giving up and renouncing their beliefs. This would also demoralize the rest of the believers. But no such occurrence took place. Blandina and Sanctus were immutable. And all the rest of the servants of God were inspired.

Among those who had denied Christ during the initial interrogations was a woman named Biblias. The devil, thinking that he had already swallowed her, and wishing to damn her still more by making her accuse falsely, brought her forth to punishment. Physically constraining the already feeble and spiritless woman, the persecutors endeavored to force her to utter accusations of cannibalism against the believers. But, in the midst of the tortures, Biblias awoke from her stupor and came again to a clear state of mind. For the temporary suffering reminded her of the possibility of eternal punishment in hell, and she contradicted the accusers of the Christians, saying, "How can children be eaten by those who do not even think it lawful to taste the blood of spiritless animals?" And then she reversed her denial and confessed herself to be a Christian – and was added back to the number of believers.

When the tyrannical tortures were found to be

insufficient to force the servants of God to renounce their beliefs, the tormentors devised other dreadful and despicable contrivances – such as confinement in the darkest and dirtiest parts of the prison, stretching of the feet to the fifth hole in the stocks, and other indignities that torturers are accustomed to inflicting on prisoners, when stirred by the devil. The result was that a great many believers expended themselves and died in prison, being chosen by the Lord for this manner of death. But there were others who were tortured so bitterly, that it seemed impossible for them to survive even if nursing had been provided. Yet they remained alive in prison, destitute of human attention, but strengthened by the Lord, and invigorated both in body and soul. These heroes consoled and encouraged all the others. But the poor souls of many of the newly converted, the just recently apprehended, and the ones whose bodies had not been previously tortured, could not endure the confinement torment, and they died in the prison.

At this time, the blessed bishop of Lyons, named Pothinus, was brought into the courtroom by soldiers of the tribunal, accompanied by the civil magistrates and a multitude of people who shouted affronts, slurs, and offences against him in every conceivable manner, as if he were the embodiment of Christ himself. He was now upwards of 90 years of age, and exceedingly weak in body. Though he breathed with difficulty on account of his body's feebleness, he was strengthened by the eagerness of his spirit to give an earnest testimony in defense of the believers. Although his body was worn out by old age and disease, the life energy was preserved within him, such that Christ might triumph through him.

When asked by the governor who the God of the

Christians was, he quietly said, "If you are worthy, then you will know and understand." That didn't go over well, and he was subsequently dragged away harshly, receiving many blows from the soldiers and the spectators. Those onlookers nearby struck him with their hands and feet, irrespective of his age, while those at a distance hurled all sorts of insults against him, each one thinking that he would be guilty of great wickedness in the eyes of the gods if he omitted any possible abuse. Sadly, they thought that by doing this, it would please their gods. Scarcely able to breathe, Pothinus was cast into prison, where he died two days later.

Now at this time, a certain great dispensation of God's providence occurred. The persecutors decided to imprison those apostates, who upon their initial arrest had denied Christ, together with all the servants of Christ who had confessed their belief, and force them to share in the confinement and hardships. Their denials, in fact, turned out to be of no advantage to them. For while those who confessed were imprisoned simply as Christians (no other accusation being brought against them), those who denied were detained as murderers – corrupted, degraded, and dishonored – and they faced punishments twice as severe. As a result, the deniers were tormented greatly by their own consciences, so that when they were led forth into the arena, their countenances were easily distinguishable from all the others, being downcast, humbled, sad-looking, and weighed down with every kind of disgrace. Moreover, they were even reproached by the local pagans as being base and cowardly. They had lost all honor, status, and reputation.

On the other hand, the confessors were lifted up by the joy of their testimony, and their hope in the promises of Christ. They went into the arena rejoicing, glory and grace being blended in their faces, so that their chains lay like sparkling ornaments around them. And they were perfumed with the sweet savor of Christ, such that they seemed to be anointed with the world's finest ointment. When they realized the fate of the deniers, they felt sorrow for them, but their hearts were strengthened knowing that the devil had no place in their own thoughts.

Then, in short order, all the accused were paraded into the arena and forced to endure the tortures until death overcame them. Their punishments were different, but the end result was always the same.

Sanctus and Maturus were publicly exposed to the wild beasts,[4] in order to give the heathen public a spectacle of cruelty that is commonly used for hard-core criminals. Like athletes who had overthrown their adversary several times and were now contending for the crown, they again endured the torments which beat upon them. They were dragged about by the wild beasts, and suffered every indignity which the maddened spectators demanded through cries and shouts. And finally, they were placed in the iron chair, on which their bodies were roasted until they were filled with the fumes of their own flesh. But the torturers did not stop there, becoming ever more frantic in their desire to overcome the stamina of the Christians. While the whole time, the only thing that was heard from Sanctus was the same four words, over and over again, that he had uttered at the beginning: "I am a Christian."

Sanctus and Maturus remained alive the entire day throughout the gruesome contest, presenting an extraordinary show for the arena spectators that was much different than the usual gladiatorial combats. But at last, their lives were sacrificed, their bodies broken beyond recognition. But their will and their faith were never shattered. And so, Sanctus and Maturus went to be with their Maker, our God and Creator, wearing the holy crown of martyrdom.

Attalus was in great demand by the people for a spectacle in the arena because he was a person of notoriety, one that epitomized the immorality of the Christians. He accepted the punishment with clear conscience, entering the contest readily as a true witness for Christ. In an effort to demean him to the point of utter humiliation, he was paraded slowly around the arena, a sign being carried before him on which was written, *'This is Attalus the Christian'*, causing the people to be swelled with indignation against him. The boos and hoots in the arena were deafening. But when the governor learned that he was a Roman citizen, he ordered that he be taken back to prison and kept with the other Roman citizens who were already there awaiting a final determination of their fate.[5]

Blandina was hung up fastened to a stake in the ground, and exposed as food to the wild beasts that were let loose upon her. But because of her earnest prayers, and because she appeared as if hanging upon a cross in a manner similar to our Savior,[6] she inspired the servants of God with great zeal. For in their terror with their physical eyes, they saw in the person of their sister, He who was crucified for them – and that all who believe in Him and suffer for His glory, will have eternal fellowship in heaven with God Almighty.

When none of the wild beasts would touch her, she was taken down from the stake and conveyed back to prison, thus preserved for another contest. But unrealized by the wicked torturers, this was an omen of fresh hope for the believers, encouraging them to remain strong and true to the faith – a shining light in the darkness. For though she was a feeble, pathetic, and despised woman, yet she was clothed with the great and invincible armor of Christ. She would continue to overpower the enemy, and in the course of the contest, would win for herself the crown of righteousness.

After this, there was a lull for a few days as the arena was cleaned up and readied for the next spectacle. This intervening time turned out to be uplifting to the servants of God – through their tenacity and perseverance, the immeasurable love of Christ was made manifest. For through the living, the dead were made alive – through the love of the confessors, the deniers were moved to confess. There was great joy among the believers in receiving back those who they thought had been lost. Most of those who had denied returned to the church and were reinvigorated in the faith.

Being now restored to the fold, and having their spirits uplifted, they went back to the courtroom to be again questioned by the governor. For our merciful God desires not the death of the sinner, but the repentance and penance of the sinner. This new examination took place because the emperor had decided that the accused-and-sentenced confessors should be punished, but that if any of them changed their plea and denied being Christian, then they should be set free.

Now, at this time, a public festival was beginning, that was attended by crowds of people from all over the empire. The governor had the confessors, the blessed servants of God, brought to the judgment podium set up in the arena, exhibiting them as a theatrical show to the unruly spectators. And they were examined and questioned again. Those who refused to deny were sentenced to death by beheading if they possessed Roman citizenship. If they were not Roman citizens, the sentence was death by being set out as prey for wild beasts.

The original deniers were also brought to the judgment

podium in the arena, the intent being that if they still denied, they would be set free, and that would demonstrate the benevolence of the emperor. But contrary to expectations, most of them now confessed, and were added to the group of believers, where they were brought back to the church. Unfortunately, there remained a few who continued to deny. They had lost their faith and their love of God – love of self had taken precedence. They continued to disparage the servants of God by giving false reports and blaspheming the Christian way of life. May God have mercy upon their souls.

Present at these examinations was a man named Alexander, a native of Phrygia,[7] and a physician by profession. He had lived for many years in Gaul, and had become well known for his love of God and his boldness in proclaiming the truth. He stood near the judgment podium, and encouraged (by hand and body signs) those who had denied to confess. But the people were becoming angry because so many of those who had formerly denied, were now confessing. So they cried out against Alexander, as if he was the cause of their change of heart, demanding that he be removed. Sensing the tension in the air, the governor summoned Alexander before him, and inquired just who he was. When Alexander replied that he was a Christian, the governor became angry and summarily condemned him to the wild beasts. He was scheduled for the next day in the arena along with Attalus, who the governor wished to expose again in order to gratify the boisterous crowd.

And the next day the two servants of God were tormented in the arena with all the instruments devised for that unholy purpose. After having undergone exceedingly severe tortures, the pair were at last slain, to the delight of the crowd. Alexander neither groaned nor shrieked in any manner, but communed in his heart with God until the end.

But when Attalus was placed on the iron chair, and the fumes rose from his burning flesh, he shouted to the people in the crowd, "Listen to me – what you are doing here is devouring people, but we Christians do not do any such thing, or any other wicked thing for that matter." Then, some people in the stands who were smirking asked him, "What is the name of your god?" And Attalus replied just shortly before expiring, "God has not a name like mortal people have."

On the last day of the gladiatorial shows, Blandina was brought in again along with Ponticus, a boy of about 15 years of age. The two had been taken every day to the arena to watch the tortures that the others had to endure, and they were pressured to renounce their faith at every opportunity. But because they remained steadfast in their confessions, the raucous crowd became incensed – and they had no pity for the youth of the boy nor respect for the sex of the woman.[8]

Accordingly, the torturers put them through all the terrible sufferings, and inflicted upon them the entire gamut of tortures; exposing them to every brutal terror, repeatedly trying to compel them to deny their faith. But they failed. In the end, encouraged and reassured by his sister-in-Christ, and after nobly enduring every kind of inhuman cruelty, Ponticus gave up the ghost and went to be with his Maker in heaven.

The blessed Blandina was the last of them all to suffer through the array of tortures and torments orchestrated by the devil and inflicted on the servants of God. After having been like a noble mother encouraging her children to remain strong, keep the faith, love God with all their hearts, and anticipate the resurrection and eternal life in heaven, she too had to face the end game. And this she did with grace, honor, and integrity, never yielding an inch to the servants of the devil. In progression, she was scourged with whips and rakes, mauled by wild beasts, and roasted in the iron chair. Finally, she was enclosed in a net and thrown onto the horns of a frenzied bull. Her body gored, pierced, and broken apart from being tossed wildly about, she was at last impaled in a most horrific manner.

The heathens themselves acknowledged that never among them had a woman endured so many and such terrible tortures.

Thus, the heroic Blandina was the last of the martyrs of Lyons to receive a crown of righteousness. To the very end, her faith, hope, and love for Christ never wavered. She knew that the others were looking to her for inspiration and encouragement, and she knew that she couldn't let them down. Even during the final excruciating moments of torture, her thoughts were not on the pain, but on the role of helper that had been entrusted to her by God – how her purpose in life was to provide comfort and assistance to others in helping them find their way to the Light through a maze of darkness – to find the true path to God, salvation, and everlasting life, even when hopelessness and despair appeared to be overwhelming obstacles.

Martyr, saint, virgin, slave: Blandina was all of the above. In her 16 odd years of life on earth, she achieved the fullest measure of sanctity, rising from an earthly state of paucity to a divine state of abundance.

Alas, the story of what happened here is not yet complete. Even after the close of the spectacle, the madness was not yet ended, and the cruel hatred was not yet appeased. The fact that the persecutors had been rebuffed in their attempt to force the believers to renounce their faith, did not put them to shame, but rather just intensified their anger. Both the officials and the people continued to exhibit an unjust hatred of the servants of God, in fulfillment of the Scripture: "Let the wicked continue in their wicked ways, the depraved in their depravity! The virtuous must live on in their virtue and the holy ones in their holiness!" [9]

The directed violence of the persecution found another evil opportunity in the dead bodies of the believers. They threw to the dogs those who had been suffocated in prison, carefully watching them day and night, so that the bodies couldn't be retrieved and buried. They laid out the mangled remains left by the wild beasts and the scorched remains left by the fire. In like manner, they placed the heads of the decapitated next to their bodies, and left them lying unburied for many days, watched by a military guard. There were some passersby who cursed and spat at the remains, seeking to get from them further vengeance. Others laughed, mocked, derided, and insulted them, at the same time propping up their own idols, and giving them the credit for punishing the Christians. There were also people of a milder disposition, who seemed to sympathize, but they could usually be heard muttering, "So where now is their God, and what good has their religion done them? Why would they choose this in preference to their life?" Such was the thinking that characterized the conduct of the heathens.

But our state was one of deep sorrow because we could not bury the bodies of the martyrs. The darkness of night aided us not – the guards were too vigilant. Bribery failed to persuade – the little money that we had wasn't enticing enough. And pleading and begging was to no avail – the guards had been commanded, under penalty of death, to keep the watch. The officials believed that their final victory over the Christians was in not allowing the remains to be buried.

The bodies of the martyred servants of God, after

having been mistreated in every possible manner, were left exposed in the open air for six days, accessible to the grisly pickings of birds and scavengers. Then they were burned with fanfare and reduced to ashes. Unquestioning workers swept all the ashes into the river Rhone, which flows past, such that no trace of them might appear on the earth.

They did these things so as to prevent the martyred souls from being resurrected (which they had been told would occur), and then snatching victory from defeat – having the last laugh, so to speak. Even though they scoffed at the idea of a resurrection, the pagan officials had to cover all the bases – they couldn't allow any chance happening, no matter how unlikely, from seizing their victory away from them. They had to make absolutely sure that the vile Christian religion was crushed for good. While all of this was going on, they could be heard snickering, "Now let us see if they will rise again, and if their God is able to help them by delivering them out of our hands."

I am writing this letter to make sure that the world remembers these events, learns from them, and is changed for the better, in the name of Jesus Christ, our Lord and Savior. And so, altogether, 50 believers and servants of God were crowned with martyrdom in Gaul at this time, but Blandina, the virgin slave, was the most heroic of them all. In the Name of the Father, and of the Son, and of the Holy Spirit, may they rest in peace forever and ever. Amen.

May God have mercy on the world.

Your humble servant in Christ.

< *signature appended* >

[end of letter]

NOTES

————————————————

1. At the urgings and persuasions of empirical bureaucrats, many people from the Roman towns and cities in Asia Minor relocated to France to help bolster the economy there, and to present a stronger front to the barbarians of the north (the Germans and Burgundians being the greatest threats) who might have ideas about incursions into the territory of the empire. Many of the Christians in the area of Lyons had family roots in Asia Minor, where they had originally been Christianized. Pergamum was an ancient Greek city in Mysia, about 16 miles from the Aegean Sea. It is now the modern town of Bergama in the province of Izmir in Turkey.

2. Compare this to Jesus' answer to the duplicitous spies in Luke 20:20-26.

3. John 16:2

4. They first were compelled to run the gauntlet, a track filled with traps, tricks, tortures, and torments, which was the custom at the time, before fighting with the wild beasts.

5. The governor had written to the emperor questioning what the policy was for dealing with the Christians, and was awaiting an answer.

6. In Roman society, crucifixion was the usual form of punishment commonly inflicted upon slaves and the worst criminals. Roman citizens, no matter how wicked, were exempt from this indignity.

7. Phrygia was a large inland district of Asia Minor, comprising most of the central Anatolian plateau. Much of it was annexed to the Roman province of Asia in 116 BC, but some portions were incorporated within the provinces of Galatia and Cappadocia.

8. Although Blandina and Ponticus were approximately equal in age, Blandina was clearly much more mature. In fact, Ponticus looked up to her as an older and wiser sister.

9. see Revelation 22:11

3 THE STORY OF PERPETUA AND FELICITAS OF CARTHAGE

Saint, Martyr, Mother, Slave

<< *Salutation and Opening of a Letter to the Faithful* >>
(see Introduction)

The citizens and officials in the areas surrounding the great city of Carthage in North Africa, spurred on by the devil, have instigated an attack on the blessed followers of Christ, that have left us saddened beyond words. But at the same time, we have become stronger as a community because of the strength and fortitude of our holy believers, both those who stood firm against the accusers face-to-face, and those who encouraged and supported them from afar. It's difficult for me to describe the terrible sufferings that have been imposed upon us, but believers everywhere need to know what happened here, so they can understand and prepare for similar onslaughts in the future. But our will is unbreakable. Because the anguish we suffer in this world, is nothing compared to the glory that awaits us in the next.

In Carthage, we had a vibrant Christian community that included a great and wise man named Tertullian.[1] Those drawn to our growing church came from all backgrounds; young and old, rich and poor, slave and free. The Roman emperor, Septimius Severus, had forbidden conversion to Christianity or Judaism, and the local governor, Hilarianus, seeking self-advancement in the eyes of the emperor, decided to enforce this edict. Out of the blue, five of our holy believers were arrested, in clear violation of the emperor's edict, since they all were only catechumens (people preparing for baptism), and not yet officially converted. The three men arrested were named Saturninus, Secundulus, and Revocatus, a slave. The two women arrested were named Vibia Perpetua, 20-year-old daughter of a prosperous provincial family, and Felicitas (nicknamed Felicity), a slave. Perpetua had just given birth to a baby son only two weeks earlier, and Felicity was eight months pregnant. Yet no leniency was afforded either of them because of their conditions. Another Christian who voluntarily turned himself in and joined the small group, was named Saturus, their instructor in the faith.

Perpetua's pagan father was frantic with worry and tried to talk her out of her decision. As a well-educated, high-spirited woman, she had every reason to want to live – including the infant who she was still nursing.[2] But her answer was simple and clear. Pointing to a water jug, she asked him, "See that water jug over there? Can you call it by a name other than what it is?"

"Of course not," her father answered.

To which she responded, "Neither can I call myself any name other than what I am – a Christian."

This answer so upset the father that he moved angrily toward her as if to strike her. But he caught himself at the last moment, stepped back, shook his head, and stormed off in a huff.

Just before being taken to the holding prison, the five catechumens were baptized in our faith. It was a deep source of encouragement for them all. Perpetua was known for her gift of receiving messages from God and relating them to others. After the baptism, she said that she was inspired by the Spirit to ask for only one thing – endurance for all in the face of their trials and sufferings.

A few days later, the holy believers were moved to the prison, a terrible place – dark, dirty, hot, and crowded with criminals and traitors. The guards and soldiers pushed and shoved them around without any concern, just like all the others. It was a dungeon. Felicity was in much discomfort, suffering from the stifling heat, overcrowding, and rough handling while being eight months pregnant. But she remained stoic.

The next day, two deacons of the church, Tertius and Pomponius, bribed the prison guards to allow our righteous captives to be moved to a better part of the prison, where they could have visitors. Perpetua's mother and brother were able to come and bring her baby to her, and she was comforted. She was even given permission to keep the child with her in prison for a day, although I think she was pained because she felt her mother and brother suffering out of pity for her, and the trials she would have to endure.

Her brother then said, "sister, you are greatly privileged; surely you might ask for a vision to discover whether you are to be condemned or freed."

Perpetua promised that she would speak to the Lord. This she did – and her resulting vision was revealed to all the believers.

< see Appendix II for the narrative of Perpetua's dream, part 1 >

After listening to Perpetua's dream, the believers knew that suffering was their fate, and that from then on, there was no hope left for them in this life – all their hope was now in the next life.

A few days later, Perpetua's father came to visit her, worn with worry, and attempted to convince her to renounce her confession. She remembered the interaction very vividly because it was very emotional. She told it all to the others, and these were her words:

"My father pleaded with me. 'Daughter,' he said, 'have pity on my grey head – have pity on me your father – if I deserve to be called your father, if I have favored you above all your brothers, if I have raised you to reach this prime of your life. Do not abandon me to be the reproach of men. Think of your brothers, think of your mother and your aunt, think of your child, who will be missing you once you are gone. Give up your pride! You will destroy all of us! None of us will ever be able to speak freely again if anything happens to you.'

"This was the way my father spoke out of love for me, kissing my hands and throwing himself down at my feet. With tears in his eyes, he no longer addressed me as his daughter, but as a woman. I was sorry for my father's sake, because he alone of all my kin would be the most unhappy to see me suffer. I tried to comfort him by saying, 'It will all happen in the prisoner's dock, as God wills – for you may be sure that we are not left to ourselves but are all in His power.'

"Unable to persuade me to change my conviction, he left in great sorrow."

Two days later, our respected accused were suddenly hurried off for a hearing. Word had spread throughout the neighborhood that a special event was to be held at the Forum, and a huge crowd had gathered. The believers were escorted, one by one, up to the prisoner's dock, a station with an elevated step in plain view of all the crowd. In turn, each was questioned, and without a second thought, each confessed to being a Christian.

When Perpetua's turn came, her father jumped out of the crowd with her son in his arms, pulled her off the step, and begged, "Recant your confession – perform the sacrifice – have pity on your baby!"

Hilarianus, the governor, said to her, "Have pity on your father's grey head; have pity on your infant son; offer the sacrifice for the glory and welfare of the emperor."

"I will not", Perpetua replied.

"Are you a Christian?" said Hilarianus.

'Yes, I am,' she said.'

When her father persisted in trying to dissuade her, Hilarianus became exasperated and ordered him to be thrown to the ground and beaten with a rod. I'm sure Perpetua felt sorry for father, just as if she herself had been beaten.

Then, sentence was passed on all the holy believers. They were condemned to death in the arena – to do battle with the wild savage beasts – and were then returned to the prison. Perpetua asked that her father bring her the baby, so she could continue with the nursing, but he refused, and she was grieved.[3]

In addition, Felicity was greatly troubled, both physically and spiritually. The labor pains were increasing and the day of birth was drawing near, but it was against the law for pregnant women to be executed, since killing a child in the womb was like shedding innocent and sacred blood. Felicity was afraid that she would not give birth before the day set for execution. In that case, she would likely be separated from her companions, and they would go on their glorious journey to heaven without her. Worse yet, she might have to shed her holy, innocent blood at a later date – this time along with common criminals, thieves, and deserters. She was very distressed. The other believers were worried that they might have to leave such a good friend and fellow believer behind, and then have her go into the arena later without their support.

A few days later, the warden in charge of the prison, named Pudens, had a change of heart, and began to show more kindness and respect to the holy believers, thinking that they possessed some great power from the gods. He allowed many visitors to see them for their mutual comfort. It was at this time that I was privileged to meet these heroes in person.

However, the military officer in charge was not so inclined. He treated them with contempt and harsh words because he had listened to foolish people, stirred by the devil, who warned him that they could be magically whisked out of prison by spells and incantations from sorcerers of their cult. He refused to move them to cleaner quarters.

Perpetua spoke to him directly. "Why can't you allow us to refresh ourselves properly? For we are the most distinguished of the condemned prisoners, seeing that we belong to the emperor. We are to fight on his very birthday. Would it not be to your credit if we were brought forth on that day in a healthier and fairer condition?"

The officer became embarrassed at her reproach, and gave the order that they were to be more humanely treated. And so, he also allowed friends and family to visit, and even to dine together.

Perpetua's father came, overwhelmed with sorrow. He started tearing the hairs from his beard and threw them on the ground. Then he threw himself on the ground and began to curse his old age, crying and wailing with very emotional and moving words. Perpetua was very sad but remained steadfast in her convictions.

Two days before the contest and execution, two events occurred that drove the believers from the depths of despair to the heights of joy. Secundulus was called from this world to be with God in the middle of the night, while suffering from ill health, the cold, and the unsanitary conditions. Everyone was very grieved. We believe now that it was by special grace from God – that he might not have to face the final tortures.

Felicity was also suffering a great deal in her labor. So, the holy believers poured forth prayers to the Lord in one long torrent of common grief and supplication. And immediately after their prayers, the birth pains came upon her, and she went into a difficult labor. The guards derided and insulted her by saying, "If you think you suffer now, how will you be able to stand it when you face the wild beasts in the arena?"

Felicity answered them calmly, saying, "What I am suffering now, I suffer by myself. But when in the arena and professing my faith, the Holy Spirit will be inside me and will suffer for me, just as I will be suffering for Him."

And minutes later, to the ecstasy of all, she gave birth to a healthy baby girl. God is good, alleluia! One of the Christian sisters of the accused adopted her, and brought her up as her own daughter.

The day before they were scheduled to confront the beasts in the arena, Perpetua had a vision, and afterwards shared it with the group.

< see Appendix II for the narrative of Perpetua's dream, part 2 >

On that last day, the holy believers were paraded out in

front of the public for their last meal (called the free banquet). It was a feast day before the day of the games in the arena – so that the crowd could see the prisoners and make fun of them. But our holy believers turned it all around – they didn't grovel or plead for mercy – instead, they openly addressed the crowd, warned them of God's judgement (stressing the joy they would have in their suffering for Christ), scolded them for persecuting the Christians, and ridiculed those who called them atheists or perverts. They exhorted the crowd to follow their example and accept the Lord Jesus Christ.

Saturus, the teacher, said, "Will not tomorrow be enough for you? Why are you so eager to see something that you dislike? Our friends today will be our enemies on the morrow." He then added somewhat sarcastically, "But take careful note of what we look like now, so that you will recognize us in our glory tomorrow." Many of the people in the crowd were roused to think twice about the Christians, and whether their religion had any merit. It is hoped that such thinking could help lost souls find the Kingdom of God in the future.

When the day of reckoning arrived, the noble servants of God were forcibly marched from the prison to the arena. But they did not resist the deliverance. On the contrary, they seemed joyful, as though they were going to heaven – with calm faces, trembling with anticipation rather than fear. Perpetua walked with shining countenance and calm step, as a beloved of God, and as the wife of Christ – counteracting everyone's stare by her own intense gaze upwards. With them also was Felicitas, glad that she had safely given birth so that now she could fight the beasts – going from one bloody situation into another, from the birther to the gladiator, ready to wash herself again for God's glory.

They were led up to the entrance gate and the men were ordered to put on the robes of a priest – but not a holy priest of God, but rather a worshipper of the pagan Roman god Saturn. Likewise, the women were ordered to wear the dress of a worshipper of the pagan god Ceres. But the noble Perpetua vigorously objected to this:

"We came to this state of affairs of our own free will, such that our freedom would not be violated – the freedom to worship and sacrifice who and how we choose. We willingly agreed to trade our lives for our freedom – freedom to never do what you now tell us to. By condemning us, you agreed to this trade. You cannot now change the rules set forth under the laws of the Empire. Let the world know that the rule of Caesar is being abused here! We will not wear the robes of your idols!"

Perpetua's defense was so eloquent and powerful, that even the governor Hilarianus decided to relent on this issue. And the military tribunal agreed. So, they were brought into the arena in their normal civilian clothes. Perpetua then began to sing a psalm, while Revocatus, Saturninus, and Saturus began to shout sayings from Christ to the on-looking crowd. When they came before the imperial booth where Hilarianus was seated, they yelled with accompanying gestures: "You have condemned us, but God will condemn you".

At this, the throng of spectators became enraged, and demanded that they be scourged before a lineup of gladiators. This didn't faze our holy believers, as they imagined that they were sharing in the sufferings of our Lord. They endured the whippings gracefully and were then led back to the section of the arena where the wild beasts were kept.

Saturninus had maintained throughout the incarceration that he wanted to be exposed to all the different beasts, so that his crown of martyrdom might be all the more glorious. And sure enough, at the outset of the contest he and Revocatus were matched with a leopard – and then while in the stocks, they were attacked by a bear.

As for Saturus, he was matched with a wild boar. But the gladiator who had tied him to the animal was himself gored by the boar and died a few days after the contest. Saturus was dragged about but was otherwise unhurt. Then, when he was bound in the stocks and awaiting the bear, the animal refused to come out of the cage. So, Saturus was returned to the staging area.

For the two young women, the tormentors had prepared a mad heifer.[4] They were stripped naked, placed in nets, and brought out into the arena. Barely able to walk, Felicitas had to be carried most of the way, and then dropped off like a lame goat. But even this contemptuous crowd was horrified when they saw that one person was a frail delicate woman and the other was a sickly young woman fresh from childbirth. They yelled with disapproval. And so, the pair were brought back again to the staging area, dressed in unbelted tunics, and returned to the arena.

The heifer first went after Perpetua, tossed her up in the air and she fell on her back, knocking the wind out of her. Sitting up slowly, she discovered that she was not seriously injured. And then, astonishingly, she pulled down the tunic that was ripped along the side so that it covered her thighs, thinking more of her modesty than of her pain. Next, she asked for a pin to fasten her untidy hair – for it was not right that a martyr should die with her hair in disorder, lest she might seem to be mourning in her hour of triumph.

Then, getting up, she saw that Felicity had been crushed

to the ground by the beast. So, she went over to her, gave out her hand, and lifted her up. Although they were bleeding and bruised, the two proud women then stood up side-by-side, grasped hands, raised them up in triumph; and faced the spectators staunchly, looking up to heaven. The crowd cheered loudly, but they wanted more blood. So, the two were brought back to the gate for preparation for the next ordeal.

At the gate, Perpetua was met by a young man who was also a catechumen, but not yet arrested. She seemed to be in a daze, probably from a combination of the jolts from the heifer and her own pensive swooning. To the amazement of all, she said, "When are we going to be thrown to that heifer, or whatever it is?" When told that it had already happened, it wasn't until she noticed the telltale marks of the rough experience on her body and on her tunic, that she believed. Then, she called for her brother, and spoke to him together with the unarrested catechumens, saying: "You must all stand fast in the faith and love one another – do not be weakened by the suffering that we have gone through, and that we will yet go through." We were all so proud of this noble woman, and wished that we could share in her glory.

At another gate, Saturus was addressing the friendly officer they had met earlier, named Pudens: "It is exactly as I foretold and predicted. So far, not one animal has touched me. So now you may believe me when I say that I am going in there now to be finished off with one bite of the leopard." And sure enough, at that moment a leopard was let loose, and ran to attack Saturus, who had gone through the gate into the arena. Mauled by the bite of the leopard, and drenched in blood, he staggered away while the crowd roared their approval. "Well washed! Well washed!" they cried out, not understanding that to us, this was like a second baptism – this time in blood, as a sacrifice to honor our Lord and Savior.

Back at the gate, he said to Pudens, "Good-bye, my friendly jailor. Remember me, and remember the faith. These things should not disturb you, but rather strengthen you." With this, he asked the officer for a ring from his finger, and dipping it into his own wound, gave it back to him, saying, "This is a pledge that you remember what happened here, as a record of the blood shed for the faith." And officer Pudens accepted the pledge.[5]

Our blessed men had fainted from their wounds, and the gladiators made ready to finish them off by cutting their throats. But the frenzied crowd shouted for their bodies to be brought out into the open arena, so that their eyes might be the guilty witnesses of the sword that pierced their flesh and terminated their existence – and the people could readily witness the final dispensation of the hated Christians. And so, the holy martyrs were beaten back into consciousness and paraded out to the center, together with Perpetua and Felicitas.

They were all together for the last time, bloodied, broken, and bruised. Hugging one another, they sealed their martyrdom with the ritual kiss of peace. One-by-one, they took the sword in silence, looking upward without moving. Saturus was the first to die, being the oldest and the teacher.

Perpetua was the last. She screamed as she was struck on the collar bone by the sword.[6] But the wound was not fatal. The young novice gladiator didn't know what to do. He was so nervous, he could barely hold the sword in his trembling hand – it was wandering all over the place. So, in an act of utter grace, Perpetua took the shaking hand of the young soldier, and guided the sword to her throat.

It was as though so great a woman, feared as she was by the devil and the enemies of Christ, could not be dispatched unless she herself was willing.[7]

The Holy Spirit has permitted the story of this contest to be written down, to carry out the commission of our most holy saints and martyrs, and I am unworthy to add anything to it. This glorious story must be remembered exactly as it happened.[8]

O, most valiant and blessed martyrs! Truly are they called and chosen for the glory of Christ Jesus our Lord! Any man who exalts, honors, and worships God's glory should read, for the consolation of the Church, these deeds of heroism, which are no less significant than the deeds of a century ago. For these new manifestations of virtue bear witness to the one and the same Holy Spirit, to God the Father Almighty, and to His son Jesus Christ our Lord, to Whom is the power and the glory for all the ages. Amen.

May God have mercy on the world.

Your humble servant in Christ.

< signature appended >

[end of letter]

NOTES

1. Tertullian (155–240 AD) was a prolific early Christian author. He was the first writer to produce an extensive collection of Latin Christian literature and apologetics.

2. Perpetua was properly married, but her husband and her younger brother had recently died (some accounts say that the husband was out of town).

3. Perpetua had been nursing the baby, even when in the prison, and thought that she had to continue. However, in actuality, the baby's desire for breast milk had waned, so her concern for the child's welfare was relieved.

4. A heifer is a young female cow that has not yet mothered a calf. These animals had proved to be especially vicious toward human females.

5. This is not the same person as Saint Pudens, mentioned in 2 Timothy 4:21, who was baptized by Saint Peter and martyred under emperor Nero. 'Pudens' was a common Roman name meaning 'modest'.

6. Some sources say she was stabbed between the ribs.

7. Saints Perpetua and Felicity, watch over all mothers and children who are separated from each other because of war or persecution.

8. Perpetua kept a diary that vividly described her trial and imprisonment. Details describing her death in the arena were added by a friend after the horrible events. This accounting of heroic martyrdom has been highly revered by both ancient and modern Christian scholars. Her text is one of the rare surviving documents written by a woman in the ancient world. Perpetua's diary was read annually in Carthage's churches for centuries. It was so influential that it was praised by orthodox and heretical Christians alike. 200 years later, the Church Father Augustine (354–430 AD) wrote sermons commenting on the young martyr's words. This account, known as "The Passion of Sts. Perpetua, Felicitas, and their Companions", was so popular in the early centuries that it was read during church liturgies. This powerful text, with its emotional and personal voice, continues to draw readers today. For reference, see: "Acts of Perpetua and Felicitas" in *The Ante-Nicene Fathers*, Philip Schaff (ed.), Marcus Dods (trans.), [Peabody, MA: Hendrickson Publishers, 1996]. Most scholars agree that Tertullian authored the work, using the prison diaries and letters of Perpetua and Saturus as resources, around 230 AD. Also see Thomas J. Heffernan, *The Passion of Perpetua and Felicity* [New York: Oxford University Press, 2012].

4 THE STORY OF THE THREE SISTERS

Agape, Chionia, and Irene

<< *Salutation and Opening of a Letter to the Faithful* >>
(see Introduction)

Citizens of the city of Thessalonica in Macedonia, which is the hometown of emperor Diocletian's once junior emperor (or 'caesar') Galerius, have initiated a harsh attack on our saintly believers and on our precious holy scriptures. It was Galerius who first persuaded Diocletian to commence an empire-wide persecution of Christians (so it is not surprising that the persecution is especially severe here).

It was just this year (303 AD) that Diocletian published an edict forbidding, under pain of death, any person to keep Christian doctrinal or liturgical books (the Holy Scriptures). Now, the believers concealed many volumes of these sacred books, but rumor spread among the citizens that certain people had obtained them unlawfully and were worshipping them. It wasn't long before seven of the faithful were accused by a pagan traditionalist of not following the edict. The names of the accused were Agape, Chionia, Irene (who were sisters), Casia, Philippa, Eutychia, and Agatho (being the only man). The seven were rounded up and brought before the provincial governor Dulcetius for trial. The official accusation was primarily, that they refused to eat meat as a sacrifice to the Roman gods, and secondarily, that they were hiding Christian books, that were supposed to have been surrendered for destruction.

Seated confidently in his court, the governor nodded to the secretary Artemesius to begin the proceedings.

"Your highness, if you please, I will read the testimony provided by the constabulary concerning several persons here present."

To which Dulcetius replied: "Let the information be read."

"Based on the information provided by the reputable citizen and senior pensioner Cassander, the constabulary presents to you six Christian women and a man, who have refused to eat meats as a sacrifice to our revered gods. They are named Agape, Chionia, Irene, Casia, Philippa, Eutychia, and the man's name is Agatho. Therefore, they are brought before you for judgment and ruling."

Turning to the women, Dulcetius said harshly, "What wretched madness is this of yours, that you will not obey the pious commands of the emperor and the caesar?" Then, without waiting for an answer, he looked at Agatho and asked more passively, "Why will you not eat of the meats offered to the gods, like other subjects of the empire?"

"Because I am a Christian," replied Agatho.

Dulcetius frowned, and then asked him again, "And do you still persist in that statement?"

"Certainly," was Agatho's reply.

Dulcetius then looked directly at Agape, saying: "What are your sentiments?"

She answered, "I believe in the true living God – and I will not lose all the merit of my life by any evil action that you may administer."

Then the governor said, "And what say you, Chionia?"

"I believe in the true living God", she answered, "and I follow His orders before any other's."

He then turned to Irene and said, "Why did you not obey the most pious command of our emperors?"

To which she answered, "For fear of offending the true living God."

"And what say you, Casia?" he continued.

" I desire to save my soul," she said matter-of-factly.

"Will you not partake of the sacred offerings?"

"By no means."

Then he turned to Philippa and said, "And as for you, Philippa, what do you say?"

"I say the same thing," she answered.

"And what is that?"

"That I would rather die than eat the food that you sacrifice to idols. I sacrifice only to the true living God."

"And you, Eutychia, what do you say?"

"I say the same thing," she replied, "I would rather die than do what you command."

The governor then took a different tact. Continuing to look at Eutychia, he asked, "Are you married?"

"My husband has been dead almost seven months now," she replied.

"And by whom are you with child?"

"By him who God gave me for my husband."

Staring very intently at Eutychia, Dulcetius then said in a very stern voice, "Listen to me closely Eutychia. For the good of your child, as well as for yourself, I strongly advise you to disassociate yourself from this folly, and resume a reasonable way of thinking. So, what do you say? Will you obey the imperial edict?"

"No, for I am a Christian," she responded, "and I only serve the one true living Almighty God."

With that, governor Dulcetius made a decision and gave a pronouncement: "Being far along with child, let the woman Eutychia be kept in prison until such time that the case can be reviewed again." It wasn't that he was altruistic. Roman law prohibited the execution of pregnant women, for the simple reason that the empire needed warm bodies.

After an hour rest break, the governor called forth Agape, and said, "Agape, what is your final declaration? Will you do as we do, who are obedient and dutiful to the emperors?"

Her answer was succinct. "I will not obey commands from the devil. Get behind me Satan! My soul will not be overcome by the evil intent driving these dialogues."

Shrugging his shoulders and shaking his head, he then turned to Chionia. "And you, Chionia, what is your final answer?"

"Nothing can change me," she replied.

The governor thought for a moment, and then said, "Do you have some books, papers, or other writings, pertaining to the religion of the impious Christians?"

"We have none now," Chionia retorted, "All that we once had has been confiscated from us."

He continued by asking, "Who drew you into this immoral persuasion?"

"The one true Almighty God," she said.

Hoping to get damaging information on other Christian subversives, he repeated the question: "Who convinced you to embrace this folly?"

But her answer was unchanged, "Almighty God, and his only Son, our Lord Jesus Christ."

That ended the questioning. Dulcetius had heard enough. After a few minutes' reflection, he issued his final verdict and sentence.

"You are all bound to obey our most glorious emperors and caesars (junior-emperors). But because you have willingly and continually despised their just commands, along with our suggestions, rebukes, reprimands, and warnings – and have had the boldness and rashness to adamantly ignore these admonitions, retaining the irreverent name of 'Christians' – and since to this very moment you have not obeyed the constables and officers who solicited you to renounce this Jesus Christ in writing – you shall receive the just punishment you deserve."

Sensing that Agape and Chionia were the leaders behind the disobedience, he then read their sentence: "I condemn Agape and Chionia to be burned alive at the stake, for having out of malice and stubbornness acted in contradiction to the divine edicts of our lords, the emperors and caesars; and who at present continue to profess the false and immoral religion of the 'Christians', which all pious people detest and abhor."

Then he added: "As for the other four, let them be confined in a secure prison until such time that I deem appropriate for reconsideration."

Two days later, our beloved saintly believers Agape and Chionia were burned to death without fanfare or ceremony. May their holy spirits forever rest in peace in heaven. Their sacrifice shall not be forgotten.

Two days after that, governor Dulcetius brought Irene back into court for further questioning. It seems that in the interim, the police had discovered some Christian books in her possession. By confronting her with this evidence, he hoped to convince her to recant and give sacrifice to the gods – or failing that, to get her to implicate other Christians, including her own father.

"Your madness to plain, my deluded child, since you have been found keeping to this day many books, pamphlets, and tracts unique to the ungodly Christians. You were previously required to acknowledge them when questioned thereupon, but you lied and denied that you had anything. It seems that you will not take warning from the punishment of your sisters – neither have you the fear of death before your eyes. Your punishment therefore is unavoidable.

"However, the grace of the empire is magnanimous. I will not refuse even now to make some condescension on your behalf. Therefore, notwithstanding your crime, you can be pardoned and freed from punishment, if you will yet worship the great gods of Rome. What say you then? This is your last chance. Will you obey the orders of the emperors? Are you ready to pledge obedience to the gods, and make the sacrificial offering?"

To which Irene calmly replied, "By no means will I do that – for those that renounce Jesus Christ, the Son of God, are doomed to eternal fire."

Giving up on the fate of Irene, Dulcetius decided to concentrate his efforts on obtaining information that could help the empire in the capture and punishment of other devout members of our 'Way', who he considered enemies of the state. So, he pressed Irene with further questions:

"Who persuaded you to conceal those books and papers from us for so long?"

"Almighty God," she responded, "who has commanded us to love him even unto death. Therefore, we will not betray him – we choose to suffer any punishment whatsoever, rather than allow our sacred writings to be confiscated and defamed, belittled, or destroyed."

The governor continued to press. "Who knew that those

writings were in the house?"

"Nobody, but the Almighty, from whom nothing is hidden. We concealed them even from our own servants, lest they should expose us and accuse us."

"Where did you hide yourselves last year, so that you couldn't be found when the virtuous edict of our emperors was first announced?"

"We went into the mountains, where it pleases God."

"And with whom did you live?"

"We were out in the open in makeshift shelters, sometimes in one place, and sometimes in another."

"Who supplied you with bread?"

"Almighty God, who gives food to all flesh."

"Was your father privy to this?"

"No, he had no knowledge of any of it."

"Which of your neighbors knew about this?"

Irene's response was stiff-lipped: "Inquire yourself in the neighborhood, make your own search, and draw your own conclusions."

But Dulcetius persisted. "After you returned from the mountains, as you say, did you read those books to anybody?"

"They were hidden in our house, and we dared not touch them and open them. Because we could not read the holy words day and night as we had been accustomed to doing, we were greatly distressed and anxious. We became distraught and troubled."

Realizing that he could not extract any useful incriminating information from her, governor Dulcetius issued his final sentence: "Your sisters have already suffered the punishments for which they were condemned. As for you, Irene, since you were condemned to death before this latest crime of hiding these books before the just eyes of the empirical magistrates, your punishment must be greater and entail even more suffering. You do not deserve to die quickly or mercifully. Therefore, I order that you be left exposed naked in a brothel, and open to whatever depravities exist in that place. You are allowed only one loaf of bread a day, and the guards will prevent any escape from your cell, under penalty of death to them."

Irene was led away to a low-end brothel to serve her sentence. As per the decree, she was left naked in a cell and subject to all the worst debaucheries imaginable. Many wicked unscrupulous men, and even some women, came to her cell. But in all cases, no matter how offensive, depraved, or licentious the intruder was, Irene enraptured and mesmerized them with a saintly radiance that was gifted to her by God. None of them felt compelled to force any immoral or indecent advances on her, and they all left the cell contented – praise the lord – thanks be to God.

After three days, the governor caused her to be brought again before him

"Do you still persist in the rashness of your beliefs?" he asked.

"Not in rashness of belief, but in eternal belief of total piety towards God," she replied.

"Then it is settled," decreed the governor, "You shall suffer the just punishment for your insolence and obstinacy."

Then he imposed the official sentence: "Since the woman Irene will not obey the emperor's orders and sacrifice to the great gods of Rome, but, on the contrary, persists still in the irreverent and wicked religion of the 'Christians', I order her to be immediately burned alive, as her sisters have been."

That very day, she was seized by the soldiers of the court

and brought to a high mound of ground where the executions were commenced. Having lighted a large pile, they ripped off her clothes and tied her to the stake. Singing psalms and celebrating the grandeur of God, the glorious martyr Irene was there-and-then consumed in the fiery inferno. Now she is with our Lord and God in heaven. May she rest in peace, the saintly Irene.

These events occurred in the ninth term of emperor Diocletian, and the eighth of caesar Maximian, to which I attest as an outside but informed party to the events.

May God have mercy on the world.

Your humble servant in Christ.

< signature appended >

[end of letter]

5 THE HEROIC SLAVE WOMEN

Saint, Martyr, Slave

MARRIED or unmarried, the female slave deserves a special place in martyrdom history. Rising from the very bottom to the very top required a massively strong inner strength and conviction. Faith, freedom, and virtue, equally threatened, were overcome by saintly passion and surrender. To recognize them is to admire them. But to remember them is to honor them.

THE FORGOTTEN HEROES

Seraphia of Rome (~119 AD)
(see chapter 1)

Zoe of Pamphylia (~127 AD)
(see chapter 1)

Ariadne of Phrygia (~130 AD)
Ariadne was a slave in the household of a prince of Phrygia, a Roman province in central Anatolia (modern-day Turkey). Because of her Christian faith, she refused to participate in sacrificial rites to a pagan god, as part of the prince's birthday celebration. Because of this, she was beaten

and handed over to Roman officials on charges of disobedience to her owner and disrespect to the gods. But she managed to free herself from the officials holding her and ran away from the household into the countryside. Of course, she was pursued by the authorities, and eventually found in a hilly glen not too far away. Just as she was about to be apprehended, she fell into a tiny hollow in the ravine and was never seen again – the assumption being that she was entombed in the rock.[1]

Agathoclia of Aragon (~230 AD)
(see chapter 1)

Sabina the Slave (~250 AD)
In an act of punishment and intimidation for failing to properly revere the Roman gods as commanded, a Christian slave named Sabina was bound and abandoned in the nearby mountains by her pagan mistress, who was attempting to 'teach her a lesson'. The owner wanted to change the girl's way of thinking (her faith) and force her to be more obedient. The plan was to let her suffer for a few days and then bring her back, humbled and changed from her old ways.

But Sabina freed herself and hid to prevent recapture. Searchers were sent to find her, but she didn't want to go back – she didn't want further punishment, but she didn't want to change her religious convictions either. She kept running and hiding, just out of reach of the pursuers. She was fortunate to find a friendly underground Christian community who secretly gave her food and money. They even contacted the pagan owner and made heroic efforts to legally free her from her bondage and servitude. But the mistress was resolute and hired bounty hunters to find not only her servant, but also the underground Christians. The search was relentless, and eventually Sabina was found and the Christians scattered.

The owner then had Sabina brought before the official prosecutors, with hopes that she would repent. But Sabina would not give in to her evil mistress or to the cruel threats from the judge. In the end, she was found guilty and convicted. Torture followed as expected and Sabina expired quickly. She willingly chose death as a martyr rather than subjugation to the pagan mistress with her pagan gods. Instead, she chose the glorious life in heaven in service to Jesus Christ.[2]

Basilissa and Kalliniki (~252 AD)

A wealthy Christian widow in the Roman province of Galatia,[3] Basilissa wanted to give money to the Christians who were incarcerated in prison there for their faith. Although not allowed to give food or clothing, it was possible to slip them some money during visiting hours when no one was looking. This would give them encouragement and hope for the future. In turn, they could slip it to their families or to the church, along with their prayers. Basilissa knew that many of these prisoners were destined for martyrdom, and they needed understanding and reassurance. Clipped to the currency bills was a note that said, "Stay the course – your reward will be in heaven."[4]

Basilissa would give the money (along with instructions) to her young servant girl Kalliniki,[5] who would go to the prison and secretly distribute it to the Christians who were confined there.

One day, Kalliniki was discovered and arrested. They asked her why she was giving money to the prisoners, since it was illegal. She said that it was for their future in heaven. This didn't make any sense to the authorities, so they asked her who had told her to do this. Unable to lie, Kalliniki told them that her mistress had given her the money. Then, she was tied up and thrown in a jail cell. Naturally, they found Basilissa a short time later and she also was arrested.

The next day, the two women were brought before the judge in court and charged with abetting the prisoners. But both women boldly confessed that they were Christians, and had a duty to help fellow Christians in need. Very quickly, they were found guilty of not worshipping the gods, and were sentenced to various tortures, in an attempt to make them deny their faith.

However, under the protection of God, the tortures were ineffective and neither Basilissa or Kalliniki could be persuaded to renounce their faith or to offer a penitent sacrifice to the pagan idols. Consequently, they were both beheaded by the sword that very day. May their souls rest in peace in the Kingdom of Heaven.

Flora and Lucilla of Rome (~260 AD)

Sisters Flora (also known as Fiora) and Lucilla were two of 23 Christians martyred together in Rome in the persecutions of emperor Gallienus. They had been kidnapped and enslaved by Saint Eugene of Rome before his conversion to Christianity, but were freed after his conversion.

Julia of Troyes (~273 AD)

Julia was captured as a spoil of war by the forces of Roman emperor Aurelian following their victory over Tetricus. She was given as a prize to Claudius of Troyes, France, an army officer. However, she converted him, and they were martyred together by beheading.

Mary the Slave (~300 AD)

Mary was a hard-working Christian slave in the house of Tertullus, a pagan patrician in Rome. She was accused and delivered to the local governor on charges of being a Christian during the persecutions of emperor Diocletian. Despite Tertullus' valiant efforts to save her, Mary suffered so many horrible tortures that local citizens demanded that she be released. The governor then turned over the custody of her to a soldier who he thought needed a slave, even though she was considered 'damaged goods'. However, the soldier helped her to escape from the city and disappear into the mountains. Legend has it that she lived a long life and died a natural death. However, she is venerated as a martyr because of the intensity of her sufferings and intention to sacrifice her life.

Laurentia of Ancona (~302 AD)

Laurentia was the wet nurse or slave, of an aristocratic Roman woman living in Ancona, Italy, named Palatias (Palatia). Laurentia converted her mistress Palatias, to Christianity, and they were both martyred in Fermo, Italy, during the persecutions of emperor Diocletian. The story of their lives and martyrdom contain many of the same legendary tales as found in the accounts of other virgin saints, such as Saint Christina and Saint Barbara. A church and a monastery were built in their honor in Ancona.[6]

Engratia, Julia, and the Martyrs of Zaragoza (~303 AD)

Engratia was a native of Braga, Spain, who had been promised in marriage to a nobleman of Roussillon in Gaul. Escorting her from Braga to Gaul was her uncle Lupercius,[7] a suite of 16 noblemen, and a servant girl named Julia (or Julie).

Upon reaching Zaragoza (Saragossa), they learned of the persecution of Christians there by a man named Dacian, who was the governor of the region during the reign of co-emperors Diocletian and Maximian. Engratia obtained a hearing before the governor, where she attempted to dissuade him from his persecution. But Dacian was not willing to listen, and instead had her whipped and imprisoned. When it was discovered that she was a Christian, she was tortured severely. She died of her wounds in prison. Julia and the other travelling companions were all beheaded as Christian accomplices.

Many others, called the 'Martyrs of Zaragoza',[8] were martyred during this time of intense persecution.

Devota of Corsica and Monaco (~303 AD)

A young Corsican woman who had decided to devote herself fully to the service of God, Devota became a servant or slave in the household of the Roman senator Eutychius. When the governor Barbarus arrived in Corsica with a fleet of ships, he learned that the senator was harboring a Christian in his house. He demanded that she be given up and compelled to perform the requisite sacrifice, but Eutychius refused. Not wanting to confront him directly, Barbarus simply had him poisoned. Devota was then imprisoned and tortured for her faith – her mouth crushed, and her body was dragged through rocks and brambles. She was eventually executed by being racked and stoned to death.

After her death, the governor ordered for her body to be burned to prevent its veneration. However, it was saved from the flames by local Christians, who placed the body on a boat bound for Africa, where it was believed it would receive proper Christian burial. However, a storm overtook the boat, and it was guided (some say by a dove) to the present-day port of Les Gaumates, in the Principality of Monaco.[9]

Leocadia of Toledo (~304 AD)

Leocadia was a young slave who was beaten and imprisoned for refusing to denounce her faith during the persecutions of emperor Diocletian. Scheduled for torture, and then either apostasy or martyrdom, she learned of the abuse being suffered by a 13-year-old girl in Merida, Spain, named Eulalia.[10] Leocadia could not bear living in a world where such evil occurred, and so she prayed to God to remove her from this world and all the evil in it. She died shortly thereafter, of unknown causes without having to face the torturers. She is considered a saint because of her strength of faith and prayer, and is thought to have been called to heaven supernaturally.

Charitina of Amisus (~304 AD)

(also known as Charitina of Rome)

Distinguished by her strict chastity and piety. Charitina spent her life in fasting, prayer and study. Orphaned young, she was the servant of an eminent Christian man called Claudius the pious, who brought her up as his own daughter. The young woman was very pretty, sensible, and kind. She imparted her love for Christ to others, and by her example she converted many to the true way of salvation. Charitina was meek, humble, obedient and silent. Although not as yet baptized, she was a Christian at heart, and studied the law of God day and night. She vowed to live in perpetual virginity as a true bride of Christ.

However, word got out that she had Christian leanings

and was bringing others to the Christian faith. The regional governor, Dometius, heard about her and sent soldiers to forcibly seize her from her home and bring her to trial.

In the courtroom, the judge asked her: "Is it true, little girl, that you are a Christian, and that you delude others by bringing them to this dishonorable religion?" To this, Charitina courageously replied:

> *It is true that I am a Christian, and a lie that I delude others. I lead those in error to the Way of Truth, bringing them to the Path of Christ.*

The judge was not amused. He ordered that her hair be cut off and hot coals be dumped on her head, but the maiden was preserved by God's power. They threw her into the sea, but by God's will she swam to shore and stood up, exclaiming, "Now I have been baptized." She was bound to a torture wheel which began to turn, but by God's word the wheel jammed, and Charitina remained unharmed. Then the wicked judge sent some dissolute youths to rape her. Fearing this dishonor, Charitina prayed to God to receive her soul before these vile men could foul her virginal body. And thus it was: while she was kneeling in prayer, her soul went out from her body to the immortal Kingdom of Christ. The angry heathens desecrated her body and then threw it into the sea. But Charitina had died a martyr's death and was one with God in heaven.

Maxima of Rome (~304 AD)

Maxima was a nurse/slave in Rome who secretly baptized Saint Ansanus.[11] She was scourged, along with Ansanus, for stealing and secretly burying the body of Saint Lucy and for professing Christianity, during the persecutions of emperor Diocletian. Maxima died from the scourging, but Ansanus lived and went on to evangelize in Siena, Italy.

Ligna, Eunonia, and Eutropia (~304 AD)
(The Slaves of Saint Afra)

It is not expressly known whether these slaves had been converted to Christianity before execution, or whether they were just following direction from their owner. In truth, it may have been a little of each. They were probably present when Bishop Narcissus of Augsburg converted Afra and her mother Hilaria, and heard the sermonizing; or they may have been subsequently evangelized by Hilaria or Afra; or they may have just listened, nodded, and then ignored everything that had been said. Like most slaves, it would depend on the personal relationship they had with their master, along with their own inner convictions.

Dula the Slave (~307 AD) (also called Theodula)

The virgin martyr Dula was the Christian slave of a pagan soldier in Nicomedia, Asia Minor. She died by stabbing, fighting off a rape attempt by her evil owner.

NOTES

———————————————

1. Legend has it that a crack in a large rock opened up just wide enough for her to squeeze into and get away. So, it wasn't a fall, it was an escape. But she was caught in the rock some distance away and couldn't get out.

2. "The Martyrdom of Pionius", in Herbert Musurillo, *The Acts of the Christian Martyrs* [Oxford: University Press, 1972]

3. A region in central Turkey, today

4. We don't know exactly what the note said. In effect, it was a plea not to lose their courage amid the coming tribulations - to not renounce the faith and lose their future life in heaven.

5. Whether Kalliniki was legally a servant or a slave is unknown, but a slave would be a good guess. Either way, Kalliniki appears to be very acquiescing to Basilissa. Putting a servant into such a dangerous situation poses many probing questions. The name Kalliniki is of Greek origin, meaning "beautiful victor", in feminine form.

6. Their relics of Laurentia and Palatias were collected in one small bronze urn, and donated to Ancona Cathedral by Pope Benedict XIV, who had been bishop of that city.

7. sometimes identified with Luperculus, who was a bishop of Eauze

8. Also called the 'Countless Martyrs of Zaragoza', there were actually two groups of martyrs. The first group consisted of 17 men and 2 women (with 2 survivors). The second group was too numerous to count.

9. The 'Legend of Saint Devota' is one of the Principality of Monaco's oldest traditions – it has influenced the national culture in fields as diverse as religion, customs, history, literature, the arts, painting, music, coins, and stamps. The legend holds a special place in the heart of Monaco's people, and over the centuries has been awarded a permanent place in the city's history.

Regrettably, many young people today only know of the name by its association with Monaco's Grand Prix Formula 1 race, and the famous 'bend of Saint Devota' that is endlessly quipped by radio and TV commentators.

10. Saint Eulalia is a venerated 12-13 year old virgin martyr from Merida, Spain (who may be the same person as Saint Eulalia of Barcelona).

11. Saint Ansanus the Baptizer, called 'The Apostle of Siena', died in 304 AD and is the patron saint of Siena, Italy.

COMMENTARY

IN general, Empires have better things to do than persecute monks, slaves, and nursing mothers. Powerful rulers tend not to care much about what people are doing as long as the servants are cleaning the house and cooking the food, taxes are collected, and no riots or unrest are occurring. But with regards to the cult of the Christians, something was anomalous – something weird about them. For a period of time, the persecution of Christians had been generally sporadic, local, improvised, and involved very few people. It was at the discretion of a regional governor to whom complaints were made by disgruntled citizens. It wasn't a dragnet or an imperial policy. Then, suddenly in the middle of the 3rd century, there was a policy shift. In the year 250 AD, the Emperor Decius decided that the Christian cult was a real threat to the Roman order, and that they had to be dealt with, empire-wide, with all the police power that the regime could muster. And so, he issued an official decree that everyone had to make a sacrifice to the Roman gods for the well-being of the empire. Furthermore, they also had to produce a certificate signed by a Roman official that verified that they had done so. Failure to do this, could have severe and brutal consequences.

In many places, Christianity, which had begun with tiny groups scattered in various cities across the empire, had now become a significant segment of the population. In some towns, they were even a majority. But they came palpably to the attention of the emperor because of their aloofness and counter-cultural tendencies. In the narrow view of the imperial office, these were the people who worshipped a man who had been crucified under Pontius Pilate, a Roman governor – and now they worshipped him as the son of a god, but not a Roman god. Obviously, they must be atheists, since they don't recognize the Roman gods. Furthermore, they seemed to engage in practices abhorrent to Roman customs, like incest, cannibalism, and orgies. Worst of all, they were becoming highly organized on an empire-wide basis, and not just on a local basis like other fringe religious communities. Clearly, they posed a threat to Roman stability. One can almost hear them murmuring behind closed doors something to the effect of: "This is dangerous – we can't have this large of a group doing things that could de-stabilize our society. Something has to be done about it...."

As a result of the spread of Christianity, a large number of gentiles were now claiming the same religious exemption that the Jews had long had. Years ago, the Jewish authorities had come to a legal agreement with the Emperor that they would not be forced to participate in the pagan rituals that were part of the normal fabric of life in a Roman city. They were given a religious exemption as a gesture of imperial goodwill. But a gentile who refused to participate had no legal standing. As a gentile, the proper thing to do was to honor the gods of the empire. By not doing this, the Christians made themselves conspicuous, and invited the legal action of the Roman authorities. They became symbolic 'outlanders'. And therefore, they were used as a societal relief valve whenever political, social, or economic relief was needed in society.

The Hollywood view of Christianity as a persecuted underground society that skulked around in catacombs for three centuries before finally emerging 'out of the closet' after emperor Constantine's conversion, is not entirely true. Before the year 250 AD, persecution was sporadic, small scale, and often precipitated by local issues. However, the Christians were perceived as different. They turned away from the rituals and beliefs held by the general society, both religious and civic. They did not become involved in the more visible functions of society – they became aloof. This aroused suspicion among many of the prominent citizens. "Why don't the Christians participate in the rituals that are necessary to please the gods, and keep our society under their protection?" they wondered. There was suspicion that the Christians were trying to undermine the Roman society by their behavior. "If the Christians are not doing their duty to the gods, then why should the gods do anything good for the city?" they reasoned. And that was often the rationale for dragging Christians before the governor and accusing them of being troublemakers whenever there was a blip in the status-quo.

This was a time when the emperor was under great pressure. There was a lot of internal dissension, stacks of sheer corruption in the aristocracy (from the emperor on down), rampant inflation, and incredible governmental instability (driven by assassination or coup d'état, there were sometimes two or three emperors in a year.). There was also a sense that they were being besieged on the borders – that the barbarians were coming in at any moment. The Persians were dangerous, the Germans were dangerous, the Africans were dangerous, and so on – the empire was being battered on every frontier by invading armies. There was a pervasive feeling that anything that might upset the ancient contract between the Romans and the gods, was dangerous and had to be dealt with. The Christians were felt to be an internal threat to that contract. Something had to be done.

So, the Roman leaders bring to bear all the power they have at their disposal. They say, "OK, let's hit the leaders. Let's find these guys called bishops, bring them into court, and force them to recant by making a sacrifice to the emperor. If they refuse, we'll simply eliminate them and then follow the same process with all the followers." Consequently, many bishops and church leaders started fleeing to the countryside, while others were located, arrested, and tried. Ordinary people, for the first time, were rounded up, forced to sacrifice, and required to get a certificate of sacrifice (of course, the wealthier, or less steadfast, individuals could buy a forged certificate of sacrifice by bribing an official).[1] However, some believers absolutely refused to make the sacrifice, despite multiple attempts at trying to convince them to. Those who remained adamant, and loyal to the faith to the very end, were executed (following a pre-established protocol).

The policy was implemented with different degrees of rigor in different jurisdictions and by different local officials. Some were severe and some were lax. But it was a different veil of persecution that hung over the Christians than the sporadic oppression that was endured prior to the enactment of the imperial policy. There was a constant fear that 'you could be next'. The fear lingered and did not quickly abate. A second wave of official persecutions occurred under the emperor Diocletian around 303 AD.

Nevertheless, the Christians endured, and the net effect of it all is that a new cult of martyrs now appeared in Christianity. Feeding on existing anti-government sentiment, the Christian church actually became toughened and expanded. Many outsiders were brought into the Christian fold, and the morale of the people was strengthened – martyrs had become heroes and personifications of Christ, the first martyr. Consequently, the physical enforcements of the Decian and Diocletian persecutions did not last that long.

The martyrs were a heroic minority – they didn't represent a huge popular swelling. There were not tens of thousands of people being martyred. What we have, instead, is tens of thousands of people admiring the few who were martyred. In that sense, the martyr crossed 'the line in the sand', beyond which only the most saintly could cross. They achieved a spiritual height to be admired but not necessarily copied. Sometimes, there were pagans present at these martyrdoms who were so impressed by the bravery and courage of the Christians that they came to see the truth of the religion themselves, and converted to Christianity. Overall, the stories of the martyrs had an incredible effect on the imagination of Christians – a regular person heroically witnessing to his own faith and against a hostile government – a hero emulating the life of Christ.[2] In general, the martyrdom accounts were written for other Christians to try to bolster their faith at a time of dreadful persecution – to keep up your courage in case it happened to you as well. However, the Christian leaders did not encourage people to volunteer themselves as martyrs.[3] Therefore, the general guidance from the church was that: 'It was OK not to volunteer yourself, but if you were apprehended, pressed, and really pushed to the wall, then you should not deny your faith'.[4] There were many controversies surrounding what to do about people who denied, and then later wished to confess again. Some churchmen took a very lax line: "Well, people are repentant.

We've all committed sins. They should just be forgiven and brought back in." Others took a kind of moderate line: "After a period of penance and public recantation and repentance, they should be allowed back into the church." And there were some hard-liners who thought that once you had renounced the faith by doing any one of those cowardly acts, there was no way for you to ever be a Christian again. Overall, there was a great deal of controversy among church people in this era, which went on for a long time.

After the enlightenment of emperor Constantine in 312 AD, there was an incredible blossoming of the cult of the martyrs. Shrines were built, liturgies were written, remains of the martyrs' bodies were distributed to churches, and there was an incredible desire to worship God near the relics of the martyrs. The era of the martyrs was closing (of course, sporadic martyrdom would continue for many more years),[5] but now the era of the heretics was just beginning.

Henceforth, most of the attacks on Christianity (with the exception of the Persian persecution – see Endnote 5) are intellectual in nature, as various ideological viewpoints and beliefs surface and resurface.[6] Different geographical regions were influenced to different extents by different heretical interpretations of the Gospel. Many of these challenges cut right to the core of the Christian faith, often resulting in bitter disputes (the ultimate definition of Christianity is itself challenged and debated over and over). But slowly over the years, the issues of contention are worked out (often not very amicably) and a canon of doctrine is slowly established. The Christian Church was beginning to become solidified and foundational. The 'rock' of Saint Peter had been firmly set in the ground.[7]

NOTES

_____

1. There were various responses on the part of different Christian communities. You could have your slave or servant go to the stationhouse and do it for you (but he might also be a Christian, and who knows what he might do or not do), or you could pay your slave/servant and hope that he could buy two certificates, or you could pay the magistrate for the certificate but not actually do the sacrifice, if you could bribe him into not looking, or you could just go ahead and perform the sacrifice, rationalizing it by knowing that these gods are nothing but idols anyway. There were all sorts of different ways that people dealt with this. However, some people absolutely refused to obey the ruling at all. And those are the people, the heroic minority, who ended up being martyred by the imperial forces.

2. Polycarp was the bishop of Smyrna (which today is modern Izmir in Turkey), and at a very old age he was brought up for trial and persecution. He refused all attempts to get him to sacrifice, and he was martyred around 165 AD. In many aspects, his martyrdom mimicked the martyrdom of Jesus – there is a government official named Herod who's partly responsible – he is put upon a donkey and rides into the city – pagan officials try to get him to renounce his faith – to offer a pinch of incense to Caesar to show his reverence for the Roman emporium. But Polycarp refuses to do any of these things. And so, he is put to death by burning. After his death, his father collects his bones and saves them. This is one of the first instances that reveal the cult of the martyrs – the practice of preserving bits and pieces of the bodies of martyred people and holding them in great honor and esteem. Many of the martyrdoms after the time of Polycarp follow this same basic practice.

3. There are a few accounts in the historical records where in a fit of unbridled enthusiasm, a young Christian would run into the arena and yell, "Martyr me!" But when the angry wild beast came running toward him with glistening fangs, he quickly decided this wasn't such a good idea after all, and caved in to the oppressor's wishes. This brought a definite degree of shame and disgrace to Christianity.

4. After the two major persecutions of the third century and the early fourth century, there was a serious problem for the church because many Christians were not made of the same 'right stuff' (moral fiber) as the people who went to their death as martyrs. Perhaps under duress, they had disavowed the faith – by offering a sacrifice of incense to the emperor, or by bribing the officials to give them a certificate saying that they had offered the sacrifice, when in fact they had not. All of this posed a grave problem for the church when the persecutions were over because many of these people then wanted to come

back into the church fold (this even included some bishops) – people were asking pointed questions, like "were you truly baptized if you had been baptized by a bishop who fell away from the faith during the persecutions?"

5. Intense persecution continued especially in the regions east of the right bank of the Tigris River at the frontier between the Roman and the Persian Empires. The Persian persecution under King Shapur II was severe from 337-379 AD. The Christianization of the Roman Empire was especially distasteful and disruptive to the primarily Zoroastrian people of Sasanian Iran, since a great many Christians were living in the western regions of greater Persia, and their beliefs, practices, and behavior were upsetting the societal norms, just as had happened in the Roman Empire in the previous 300 years. Altogether, the common estimate of 16,000 martyrs is considered conservative by many – it may have been much greater.

6. There were many heresies faced by early Christianity. Principle among them were Gnosticism, Montanism, Arianism, Docetism, Nestorianism, Sabellianism, Manichaeism, Donatism, Ebionites, and Marcionism. For a more complete list of all the heresies, and how the church addressed them, refer to https://en.wikipedia.org/wiki/List_of_heresies_in_the_Catholic_Church.

7. Matthew 16:18

APPENDIX I

Index of Heroes

Chapter 1: Martyrdom of Women Slaves
The Deaconesses of Bithynia
Zoe of Pamphylia
Felicitas of Carthage

Chapter 1: Martyrdom of Unmarried Women Slaves
Seraphia of Rome
Blandina of Lyons
Agathoclia of Aragon

Chapter 2:
Blandina of Lyons

Chapter 3:
Perpetua and Felicitas of Carthage

Chapter 4:
Agape, Chionia, and Irene of Thessalonica

Chapter 5: The Heroic Slave Women
Seraphia of Rome
Zoe of Pamphylia
Ariadne of Phrygia
Agathoclia of Aragon
Sabina the Slave
Kalliniki of Galatia
Flora and Lucilla of Rome
Julia of Troyes
Mary the Slave
Laurentia of Ancona

Julia of Zaragoza
Devota of Corsica
Leocadia of Toledo
Charitina of Amisus
Maxima of Rome
The Slaves of Afra
Dula the Slave

APPENDIX II

The Last Dreams of Perpetua

Perpetua's Dream, Part 1:

I saw a ladder of tremendous height made of bronze, reaching all the way up to the heavens – but it was so narrow that only one person could climb up at a time. To the sides of the ladder were attached all sorts of metal weapons – swords, spears, hooks, daggers, and spikes – so if anyone tried to climb up carelessly or without paying attention, he could easily be injured, and his flesh torn by the weapons. At the foot of the ladder lay a dragon of enormous size. It would attack those who tried to climb up, and try to terrify those who were unsure.

Saturus was the first to climb up – this gentle man who was later to give himself up of his own accord. He had been the builder of our strength, although he was not present when we were arrested. When he arrived at the top of the staircase, he looked down and called to me, "Perpetua, I am waiting for you. But take care – do not let the dragon bite you."

"He will not harm me," I said, "in the name of Christ Jesus."

Slowly, as though he were afraid of me, the dragon stuck his head out from underneath the ladder. Without hesitation, I jumped on his head, and using it as my first step, went on up.

At the top I saw an immense garden, and in it sat a gray-haired man wearing shepherd's clothes. He was tall and milking a sheep. Standing around him were many thousands of people clad in white garments. He raised his head, looked at me, and said, "I am glad you have come, my child."

He called me over to him and offered me some of the milk he was drawing. I took it in my cupped hands and consumed it gratefully. And all those who stood around said, "Amen!"

At the sound of this word, I awakened from the vision, with the taste of something sweet still in my mouth.

Perpetua's Dream, Part 2:

Pomponius, the deacon, came to the prison gates and began to knock loudly. I went out and opened the gate for him. He was dressed in an unbelted white tunic, wearing elaborate sandals.

He said to me, "Perpetua, come – we are waiting for you."

Then, he took my hand and we began to walk through the wild and rugged countryside. At last, we came to the amphitheatre out of breath, and he led me into the centre of the arena.

"Do not be afraid," he told me. "I am here, struggling with you." And then he left.

I looked around at the enormous crowd, who were watching me with astonishment. I was surprised that no beasts were let loose, for I thought that I was condemned to die by the beasts. Then, out came an Egyptian fellow of vicious appearance, together with his assistants, to fight against me. But some handsome young men also came out to stand with me, as my assistants.

Suddenly, my clothes were stripped off, and I noticed that I looked like a man. My assistants began to rub me down with oil (as they normally do before a contest). Looking over to the other side of the arena, I saw the Egyptian man rolling in the dust, preparing for battle.

Next, there appeared a giant of marvelous stature, rising above the top of the amphitheatre. He was clad in a beltless purple tunic with two stripes (one on either side) running down the middle of his chest. He wore sandals that were wondrously made of gold and silver. He carried a wand like an athletic trainer, and a green branch on which there were golden apples growing.

He commanded the crowd to be silent, and said, "If this Egyptian can defeat the woman, he will slay her with the sword. But if she defeats him, she will receive this branch of green and gold." Then he withdrew.

The Egyptian and I drew close to one another and began to let our fists fly. My opponent tried to get hold of my legs, but I kept striking him in the face with the heels of my feet. Then, he raised me up into the air, and I began to pummel him without my feet touching the ground. When I noticed there was a lull in his attack, I put my two hands together, linking the fingers of one hand with those of the other, and managed to get hold of his head. Pushing downwards, he fell flat on his face – and so I stepped on his head!

The crowd began to shout and my assistants started to sing psalms. So, I walked up to the giant and took the branch of green and gold. He kissed me and said, "Peace be with you, my daughter!" I began to walk in triumph towards the Gate of Life, but then suddenly I awoke.

It was then that I realized that the real fight in my life would be against the Devil, and not against the wild animals. I also knew that I would win the victory!

About the Author:

Edward N Brown is a storyteller with a background in science, philosophy, theology, and engineering. His technique is to blend the interesting nuggets of history, myth, science, biography, design, romance, poetry, spirituality, and personal drama – all mixed together into an informative, but easy-reading, faith-based tale of inspiration and wonder. Years of personal study exploring the great mysteries that connect the secular with the spiritual, coupled with an educational background of three advanced degrees (PhD + two MS) with a focus on systems thinking, have contributed to his insights on Reality, Ancient History, Christianity, and the Human Condition. His works represent a speculative fusion of style – one that will both entertain and inform readers of all ages.

Crystal Sea Press website: http://www.crystalseapress.com
Crystal Sea Press email: rystalse@crystalseapress.com
Amazon Author Page:
   https://www.amazon.com/author/crystalseapress_enbrown
Goodreads Profile Page:
   https://www.goodreads.com/author/show/19232863.Edward_N_Brown
Facebook Publisher Page:
   https://www.facebook.com/Crystal-Sea-Press-106797100691990/

Other Books by Edward N Brown

The Passion of Thecla: Faith and Fortitude
- 2020 Edition

The Passion of Eve: Remembering the End
- 2020 Edition

The Passion of Eve: Remembering the Beginning
- 2020 Revised Edition

The Passion of Eve: Remembering the Beginning
- 2019 Original Edition

(all books available in Paperback and e-Book formats)

"I AM the ALPHA and the OMEGA," says the Lord God,
"the One who is and who was and who is to come,
    the Almighty!"
"I AM the ALPHA and the OMEGA, the First and the Last,
    the Beginning and the End!
Blessed are they who wash their robes so as to have free
    access to the Tree of Life ..."

Revelation 1:8 and 22:13-14